# MEANING AND EXPRESSION

# MEANING

## and

# EXPRESSION

## Toward a Sociology of Art

## by Hanna Deinhard

BEACON PRESS  BOSTON

English translation copyright © 1970 by Hanna Deinhard

German text copyright © 1967 by Hermann Luchterhand Verlag GmbH

First published in German under the title *Bedeutung und Ausdruck: Zur Soziologie der Malerei*

Library of Congress catalog card number: 75–119676 ✓

International Standard Book Number: 0–8070–6664–8

Beacon Press books are published under the auspices of the Unitarian Universalist Association

Published simultaneously in Canada by Saunders of Toronto, Ltd.

Printed in the United States of America

The author gratefully acknowledges permission to quote copyright material from *A Documentary History of Art*, Vol. I, by Elizabeth Gilmore Holt, copyright 1947, © 1958 by Princeton University Press, reprinted by permission of Doubleday and Company, Inc. *Faust, Parts One and Two*, by Johann von Goethe, translated by George Madison Priest, copyright 1941 by Alfred A. Knopf, Inc., reprinted by permission of Alfred A. Knopf, Inc.

# Contents

# Illustrations

# 1.

# Timeless and Time-bound Art

"Every great work of art is timeless"; "every work of art is an expression of its time." These two well known statements provide the simplest formulation of a problem whose solution is of decisive significance for every discipline concerned with the nature, the development, or the value of art and raising the claim to scientific objectivity.

No way of looking at art that fails to comprehend the special connection between these two opposing statements can understand either the historically given variety of works of art or the creative activity that produces them. In other words: any theory that places works of art outside history, be it with regard to their origin or to their effects, can offer no explanation for the existence of the different arts, the immense diversity of works of art, nor for the fact that these works are evaluated differently at different times. (Why were architecture and sculpture the leading arts in certain epochs, and painting in others? Why did Mansart have the high altar, the choir screen, and the choir stalls in Notre Dame de Paris destroyed and replaced by others in 1699? Why were El Greco's works considered less valuable than Guido Reni's in the nineteenth century and more valuable today?)

If, however, artistic activity and the work of art are regarded solely as the expression and result of a unique set of historical conditions, there is the risk of degrading the work of art to the status of a mere example of economic, religious, social, or political forces, in which case what is specifically artistic is overlooked or remains unexplained.

The monumental work achieved during the last two or three generations by art historians and art theoreticians of the most diverse persuasions has made it possible to order the great majority of existing works of art in terms of attribution, dating, place of origin, etc. But today, after the achievements of this fundamental labor, both those who assert the absolute autonomy of art and those who maintain that art is completely determined historically find themselves in a position which can lead only to more and more pointless hairsplitting. (To be convinced of this, examine the "strictly scholarly" art historical journals. The majority of the articles are devoid of any value either from the standpoint of methodology or of seminal knowledge of benefit to the specialist in art history, the general historian, or the historian of civilization.) The situation has certainly not been helped either by present-day overspecialization and the increasingly more negligible information it produces.

But in their extreme one-sidedness the two aforementioned tendencies have been unable, all the wealth of "factual" results notwithstanding, to help contemporary society to achieve a deeper understanding of art or new insights into its significance for human existence.

Where progress in this direction has been made, it has not come from the ranks of the "professionals" in the art field in the narrower sense of the word, that is, from the university professors of art history and aesthetics, who have become increasingly more scholastically erudite, and surely not from the art critics of the press, who have become increasingly more and more shallow, but from the works of those scholars and writers who are striving for synthesis rather than for increasing specialization. This search for a synthesis is conducive to explanations rather than mere descriptions; it has led to the creation of a new discipline, one which is still in the earliest stages, but whose scientific fruitfulness is already unquestionable and of great importance: the sociology of art.[1]

"Pure" art historians and aestheticians shudder when they hear that term and the layman rightly asks, "What is the sociology of art?" Several current definitions of the modern sociology of art could be given, but it is simplest perhaps to begin by saying that the sociology of art has its logical place and its task at precisely the point designated by the opposition between the two statements "every great work of art is timeless" and "every work of art is an expression of

1. French art historians, philosophers and sociologists have been especially active along these lines. To mention only a few: C. Lévi-Strauss, P. Francastel, A. Chastel, L. Goldmann, H. Lefèbvre, J. Cassou.

its time." The point of departure of the sociology of art is the question: How is it possible that works of art, which always originate as products of human activity *within* a particular time and society and *for* a particular time, society, or function—even though they are not necessarily produced as "works of art"—can live beyond their time and seem expressive and meaningful in completely different epochs and societies? On the other hand, how can the age and society that produced them be recognized in the works? Like every discipline, the sociology of art has as its final goal the recognition and the formulation of laws, even if they should turn out to be laws which, as Gordon Allport neatly puts it,[2] "tell how uniqueness comes about." The knowledge for which the sociology of art strives can be provisionally formulated as follows: Is it possible to discover laws or principles in accordance with which the structure and form of a given society determine the structure and form of the art of this society? Conversely, is it possible to determine whether and in what way the structure and form of the art of a given epoch affect the structure and form of the society in which it exists? Finally, what contribution could the knowledge of such laws make to a deeper understanding of art and society?

It is clear that the questions concerning such principles can be solved only when the initial problem, namely that of the relationship between "timeless" and "time-bound" art, has been clarified.

The best way to approach this problem is really to look at a work of art. In the course of this book detailed analyses of concrete works, varying in style and period, will be given. The following description of the "Coronation of the Virgin" by Quarton will serve only as an example of the general direction of the investigations. More specifically, this introductory description will provide a secure basis from which a definition of the terms "meaning" and "expression"—along with their significance for the solution of the problems which have just been raised—can be developed step by step. For the same reason the description of the "Coronation of the Virgin" precedes rather than follows the citation of the extant contract in which the conditions for the execution of the painting are spelled out in great detail.

2. Gordon W. Allport, *Personality: A Psychological Interpretation* (New York: 1937) p. 194: "A general law may be a law that tells how uniqueness comes about."

# 2.

# Enguerrand Quarton: "The Coronation of the Virgin"

More than half of the picture (fig. 1)[1] is filled with large figures, richly dressed in splendid colors and assembled in rows around a center occupied by three figures larger than the others. Although neither the anatomical nor the spatial depiction of the figures includes any "non-natural" characteristics, a viewer grown-up within the Western cultural tradition would naturally assume that the scene occurs in a non-terrestrial space since most of the figures have halos and all are placed above a narrow strip of blue sky, under which are mountains, rivers, cities and people; these latter are all very small in relation to the upper half of the picture.

Whereas in the upper part of the picture the center is marked by a female figure on whose head two figures, identical as to dress and features, are placing a crown, surmounted by a dove whose wingtips touch the mouths of the two figures performing the coronation; a crucifix forms the center in the lower part. Not only is it located on the same axis as the central figure, but it also inevitably guides the viewer's eye from the terrestrial to the non-natural part of the picture. For the slender cross rises in solitude into the blue sky, high above the lines of horizon, formed by the other objects, buildings, and landscape.

Looking more closely at the terrestrial part of the picture, figures in various occupations and costumes and of differing dimensions can be seen; in addition there are many houses and other buildings shown partly from the exterior and partly from within.

1. For detailed photographs as well as the complete text of the contract to be discussed later, see Charles Sterling, *Le Couronnement de la Vierge par Enguerrand Quarton* (Paris: 1939).

4

1. *The Coronation of the Virgin* by Enguerrand Quarton [Photographie Giraudon, Paris]

Below this terrestrial region is a zone, dark and dreary in color, which is filled with very tiny and thin figures. Despite the variety of their gestures, these all give the impression of somewhat shadowlike beings when compared to the figures on the earth and particularly to those in the celestial regions.

In this brief description of the picture, as far as possible, all terms which presuppose specific *knowledge,* such as God the Father, the Son, and the Holy Ghost, names of particular saints, angel, devil, hell, monk, Pope, have been avoided. These concepts were excluded (although not completely, to avoid a description at this point unnecessarily laborious) in order to show that the painting is a vehicle of expression by its visible existence alone (through color, composition, forms, etc.), independent of any historical knowledge. The question whether and to what extent this expression corresponds to what the work originally signified or was intended to signify will be momentarily postponed. What results come from the expressive content, the exclusively visual communication?

By far the most important part of the painting is the supernatural region, both in terms of its scale in relation to the picture as a whole and of the size and number of figures shown, the splendor of color, and the realism of the details (faces, garments, etc.) This region dominates the rest of the picture in the truest sense of the word, because the eye is continuously led back to it. The link between the upper and lower parts of the painting is accomplished, as pointed out earlier, exclusively by means of the cross. If the cross were not there, there would be no connection whatsoever between the celestial splendor and the terrestrial or subterranean regions. Were this the case, the relationship mediated by the cross would then be only a kind of formal parallel between the upper and the lower regions, completely changing the expressive content of the work. Whether the almost frail delicacy of the cross is understood as an expression of the difficulties and inadequacy of human striving for the divine or as the independence of the celestial regions from the terrestrial or, conversely, as an indication of terrestrial autonomy in relation to the celestial sphere— no matter how subjectively the individual present-day beholder reacts to any given shape—the formal mediating function of the cross can neither be denied nor ignored.

In contrast to the figures gathered above the clouds, all of whose gazes and gestures are similarly focused on the center, the terrestrial scene (fig. 2) shows a great variety of objects—countryside and cities, people engaged in the most diverse activities. To the extent that a special relationship exists between these activities and the gathering in heaven, it is not discernible from the optical data alone. Rather each terrestrial scene gives the impression of being meaningful in itself, in complete contrast to the arrangement in heaven where everything is clearly subordinated to the center.

This applies especially to the representations of the people on earth and their various activities, who are united only by the common spatial framework enclosing them. For this space is clearly characterized as a unified, finite, and particular space. In comparison, the heavenly space is finite only insofar as it stops where the figures end. But by no means is it a particular and, even in the abstract sense, a unified space.

Thus the contrast between heaven and earth optically shows the predominance of heaven in size and color, the uniform subordination of its figures to a center, and the irrationality of its space. On the other hand, the earthly existence appears diverse and independent, and in a space which is rationally comprehensible.

The "subterranean" zone (fig. 3) resembles the earth inasmuch as it also shows numerous small figures. Here, however, space is much less defined in terms of spatial depth and of spatial description, and in this respect the zone resembles the ideal space of heaven more than that of earth. Likewise the movements of the figures are more subordinated to the principle of a central power than the terrestrial human activities.

The link between heaven and earth established by the cross corresponds to the link between the earth and the subterranean zone established by the figure of the angel[2] on the rock to the left of the center. The rocks and the angel also separate the small figures, striving upwards, from those who are sinking. The bearings and gestures of these figures are clearly characterized as non-independent, not resulting from their own strength, and this again constitutes a decisive

2. If only the visual aspect is under consideration, the use of the word "angel" is, of course, as incorrect as that of "halo" used earlier. For the concept "angel" implies much more knowledge than the correct paraphrase, "a human figure with wings."

2. Detail from *The Coronation of the Virgin* by Enguerrand Quarton [Photographie Giraudon, Paris]

3. Details from *The Coronation of the Virgin* by Enguerrand Quarton [Photographie Giraudon, Paris]

difference with respect to the figures on earth and in heaven. The lack of autonomy in these movements is crystal clear and thus determines the expressive character of these scenes in contradistinction to the others. Visually, however, the explanation for this lack of autonomy can be determined only by linking it to the figure of the angel who is larger in scale than the other figures. Its *particular* meaning (in the sense of Christian ideas and teachings), however, cannot be deduced from the picture as a purely visual phenomenon.

Precisely for this reason it is especially important to point out that the painting is still expressive, that is, it still conveys conceptions concerning human existence, the relation of man to man, man to nature, man to God—in short, co-ordination, subordination, dependence, finitude—even if all specific religious, historical, and social "knowledge" is excluded and consideration is restricted to the visual aspect of the picture (naturally within the framework of the Western cultural tradition). This expressive content, which rests on the visual aspect of the work, is what is commonly referred to as "timeless" in great works of art.

Used in this sense, however, the word is ambiguous and misleading in more than one way. It may lead to the notion that this expression comes into being wholly independently of the historical situation of the artist and further that it can be comprehended independently of the historical standpoint of the viewer. In addition, the word "timeless" easily conduces to the assumption that an inalterable meaning is necessarily bound up with the expression. But none of this is correct.

The concept of timelessness will be replaced here by the term "potential content." Although this concept is no less complicated than that of timelessness, it has the advantage that the misleading view that art is ahistorical (the "eternal" charm of Grecian art) is avoided from the outset. Further, the notion of potential content makes it possible, as shall be shown, to understand the changing value judgments which all works of art, even the greatest, have undergone in the course of history and which all works of art must undergo—a fact that the concept of timelessness either ignores entirely or, in any case, fails to explain.

What is the potential content? The term is to be understood as denoting that expression in a work which results solely from the means specific to each type of art. In the case of painting, the only art form under consideration here, these means are visual. Thus the potential content is that expression in a work which springs solely from its visual nature, an expression that can only be *seen* and therefore cannot be produced *in the same way* by other means (sounds, words, thought).

Apart from pure ornament and non-representational painting, to be dealt with in a separate study, the visual aspect of a work may consist of representations of endless diversity: people, animals, fabulous creatures, landscapes, objects of all kinds. The potential content includes everything that could possibly be represented in a work, but, to repeat, only with regard to its particular visual quality, and not with respect to the literary, mythological, political, theological, etc., meaning of the representation as a whole or of one of its parts. As the sketchy description of the "Coronation of the Virgin" showed, the objects represented were identified in terms of their appearance as man, animal, house, etc.—whether or not this identification is historically correct. But they were not identified as Trinity, Pope, Dove of the Holy Spirit, Church of Holy Sepulchre, etc. (The question whether such identification is in fact historically always possible will not be dealt with here.)[3]

In short, the potential content refers to the *expression* of the work, *not to its meaning*. And whereas the expression remains *relatively constant*, the meaning is subject to change.[4] The potential content is the result of the specific creative artistic process and its realm is the general or even the universal, whereas the meaning or meanings that are connected with the expression of a work in the course of time always refer to something particular and unique. The meaning or the changing meanings of a work are neither primarily nor necessarily, nor even exclusively, the result of the visible. In contrast to the potential content, the meaning exists, as it were, independently of the visual aspect of the work, as a philosophical or political idea, a religious belief, in-

---

3. In this respect, consider the difficulty in identifying the meaning of prehistoric cave paintings. Or see, for instance, E. Gombrich, "Botticelli's Mythologies," in *Journal of the Warburg and Courtauld Institute*, vol. VIII (1945) pp. 7–60.

4. Iconology concerns itself with such changes in meaning, in the main completely neglecting the question of expression.

tellectual knowledge, material or technical fact, psychological insight, etc. In short, the meaning and the expression of a work are not identical. They may coincide, but they may also contradict each other.

But who is to determine or how can it be determined whether or not the meaning and the expression contradict each other? And if such a contradiction is possible, is it then not equally possible that there may be works of art which indeed have meaning but are without significant expressive content? Or, conversely, works whose potential content is extremely strong but which are "senseless," are devoid of meaning? No meaning for whom? Expression for whom? Further, do the intensity of the expression and the clarity or lack of clarity of the iconographical meaning say anything about the quality of a work of art? These questions can be answered only when the fundamental distinction between expression and meaning has been justified both historically and methodologically and the relation between them clarified.

To avoid misunderstandings, it should be emphasized that the distinction between meaning and expression is not simply an unnecessarily complicated reformulation of the customary distinction between form and content to be found in almost all writings about art. No doubt the potential expression is a result of the visual form or, more precisely, of the visual form-relationships in the work, without which it is inconceivable. Yet this is not the kind of formalism which holds that form produces its own content. For the way the form-relationships are concretized in the work is conditioned—although not specifically determined—by the historical situation obtaining in the period of its creation. In other words, whatever artists themselves may think, the form-relationships in a work of art are always based on extra-artistic relationships. Hence the expression that results from the form-relationships, and conveyed only by them, is not a "purely formal" expression—to the extent that "purely formal" expression is not a self-contradiction, that is, nonsense. For example, in the "Coronation of the Virgin" the relationships of dominance, subordination, dependence, etc., which are "expressive," resulted from the particular dimension, colors, etc., of the painting. But the fact that the differences in dimension, the coloring, the space, etc., were given as they are, for instance, the saints being larger than the earthly figures, does not originate in the personal taste of the individual artist or the person who commissioned the painting. Rather, this fact is conditioned by the particular religious and social *structure* of the period within which and for which the work was created. Thus the general form-relationships, as they appear in the work, are based on *extra-artistic structural relationships*. The question whether it is always possible to provide an exact explanation of this very complicated relationship between artistic form-relationships and extra-artistic structural relationships will be investigated later. For the moment it is important to state that the potential content in its visibility is objectively and concretely there for the viewer: the holy figures in the "Coronation of the Virgin" are objectively larger and richer than all the other figures, whether the picture is viewed by a believer or by an unbeliever, by a man of the fifteenth or a man of the twentieth century, whether or not they are recognized as saints, and finally, whether or not the viewer knows why these figures are larger than all the others.

Why is it so important to give such special emphasis to the fact that the visual elements of paintings are objective data? And to what extent is the visual element in a picture ever really "objectively" given? Is not all vision conditioned by the historical standpoint of the viewer just as much and perhaps even more so than the artist is in his creation? Does not every man—albeit in different degrees depending on his knowledge—see with the eyes of his time? Is not everything seen colored by what is known? If this be the case, why attribute such importance to the potential content, if it is not grasped alone, but rather combined with or interpreted through sundry factors which have little or nothing to do with the visual elements?

According to the civilization and the period, the same naked female figure will be seen as a goddess of love and beauty (Venus), an emblem of sin (*Luxuria, Voluptas*), an allegory of truth, or simply a "nude." Obviously what changes in this simplified example is not the expression (potential content) of which, in this case, nothing is known. (Is the figure treated organically or mechanically, sensuously or abstractly, monumentally or minutely described?) As a visual datum, the picture does not change. What does change is the meaning attributed to the work. And the *evaluation* of the work also changes, hand in hand with the change in meaning. In any case, it *always* changes when —but *not only* when—the viewer primarily and essentially expects meaning from the work of art and comprehends the picture as a meaningful rather than as an expressive entity. But is that not tantamount to saying that whenever a work is judged on the basis of its meaning its intrinsic artistic aspect will be passed over or disregarded? In other words, does not a judgment on a picture, based on its meaning, leave out the expressive content and thus the artistic quality?

The problem is not new. Since the middle of the nineteenth century and especially in the twentieth century, whole libraries have been written to prove that it is not the meaning of a work of art that decides its quality, but rather the *way* with which it is dealt. There is no need to repeat the various arguments, which are well known. But it may be relevant to stress once more that the "what" of a picture is all too often equated with its meaning, and that this necessarily leads to misunderstandings. The "what" of a picture, the theme, the subject matter, can be, for example, still life; the meaning, *vanitas vanitatum*. The expressive content might nevertheless be the glorification of the material, sensuous beauty of the things of the world. Often the contrast between the subject matter, meaning, and expression is particularly marked in still-life paintings.[5] But the essential question remains: is it enough to say that all judgments based on meaning are not artistic judgments inasmuch as they refer to extra-artistic—moral, political, economic—values supposedly of no consequence for the artistic understanding of the works?

This conception, which at bottom is formalistic, is unsatisfactory if only for the reason that it cannot explain the various evaluations which were passed on a same work of art in the course of history. At times, works, artists or styles that suffered long periods of dislike are once again praised as "timeless"; at other times, works that were considered "timeless" fall into oblivion, indifference, or disregard. (It suffices to remember the shift in values in the judgments of Greek and Roman antiquity: from the classic period to the pre-classic and archaic periods.) To say that taste changes is obviously no explanation.

But the formalistic conception is unacceptable for another

5. Many examples of this are found in Ingvar Bergstroem, *Dutch Still-life Painting in the Seventeenth Century* (New York: 1956) and in the articles by the same author, e.g., "Disguised Symbolism in 'Madonna' Pictures and Still Life," *Burlington Magazine*, vol. XCVII (1955) pp. 303–8, 340–9, precisely because the writer limits himself to an explication of the meaning of the works.

and more important reason: despite all its emphasis on "artistic quality" it has not been able to pose the fundamental question as to whether artistic quality can be demonstrated objectively altogether in a scientific way. But the historical question concerning changes in the evaluation of works of art, and the theoretical question concerning objective art criticism are insoluble so long as the special connection between meaning and expression in the work of art is not considered and grasped. Viewed historically, the elimination of meaning as an element of art criticism cannot be justified. For in all periods of Western art—despite their immense variety—works of art were created, until the beginning of modern art (about 1850), primarily, if not exclusively, with reference to their meaning. Pictures and sculptures were conveyors of meaning, emblematic representations.[6] Although there are dangers inherent in such generalizations, nevertheless it is correct to state that modern art alone has raised expression to the fundamental and unique principle ruling the creation and evaluation of works of art.

Now, it is easy to understand that one and the same work of art undergoes completely different evaluations, depending on whether the viewer attributes crucial importance to the meaning or to the expression of the work. The more precise and specific the formulation of the meaning which the viewer expects to find in the picture or sculpture—be it a religious dogma, a political conviction, a moral imperative, or a documentary description—the more does expression in its unique visual quality become secondary. And, conversely, the more indifferent the viewer is to the particular meaning of a work, the more important perforce become the form-relationships given in the work.

6. This applies to the whole of antiquity as well as the Middle Ages. And the so-called "expressive art" of Mannerism and the Baroque is no less meaning-minded than the art of the High Renaissance. Even Romanticism, to the extent it plays a role in the fine arts, is primarily an art of meaning. The fact that Romanticism is so often adduced as a typical example of pure "expressive art" is based on a misunderstanding; the meaning which the Romantics thought they were giving to their works, in the absence of a common meaning uniting artist and society, was so personal and individual, so dependent on accidentally discovered "kindred spirits," that the excessive subjectivity made a common grasp of the meaning impossible and thus left only the possibility of interpreting the works—however vague —as personal expression. Naturally this holds true particularly for the lesser painters of the period.

This difference in basic orientation with respect to meaning or expression explains why all periods and societies that emphasize the meaning of works of art are relatively limited in their receptivity to works of other epochs and cultures. On the other hand, in all periods and societies in which works of art are considered essentially as conveyors of expression, without regard to meaning, there is a practically unlimited willingness to accept products of the most diverse cultures and periods as *works of art*. Our age offers an especially typical example of the latter attitude. The question of whether this is necessarily proof of a more comprehensive and profound understanding of art will be dealt with later.

Emphasis on expression or meaning, of course, is by no means a simple either-or question. But it must be emphasized that in this respect the basic attitude of artist and viewer is not a matter of personal taste but rather springs from a socio-historical conditioned situation in the framework of which individual taste develops. And even though in every age differences in generation, social group, occupational interest, temperament, and psychological type produce a number of different individual tendencies in taste, some of which may be in strident contrast, the greatest oppositions are still conditioned by the historical framework which constitutes the prerequisite for social and individual judgments on works of art.

Why all this insistence on the historically and socially conditioned character of the factors that constitute the basis of the general criteria by which a society, or its various representatives, judge works of art? Because it affords the possibility of understanding why judgments of the same works, artists, and styles, necessarily differ in the course of time. In other words, because this fact provides an answer to that question which, as pointed out earlier, the formalistic and iconological conceptions of art can neither solve nor even pose.

Thus a basic relation is posited between the changing criteria of art criticism and the changes in the function or functions that art (or a particular category of art) actually fulfills (or is expected to fulfill) within a given society. Changes in the function of art produce changes in the criteria of art evaluation, among which the problem of meaning and expression occupies a special place. There is no end to the variety of such criteria: criterion of precious materials, of rarity, novelty, of preference for a particular artistic tradition or a particular subject matter (landscape, portrait, history painting, etc.); all have constituted (and in many cases continue to constitute) criteria which not only influence the evaluation of works of art but even their specific form.

It appertains to general sociology to investigate, in collaboration with art history, changes in the function of art and their consequences for changes in "taste" and criteria of judgment. (It hardly needs mentioning in this context that great works of art have been created within practically all social and economic systems.) But in order for the results obtained by this type of investigation to make a significant contribution to the understanding of art, they must be complemented by an analysis which poses the question of artistic quality with regard to individual works as well as to general stylistic tendencies (archaic, classical, etc.). Yet neither general sociology nor art history can pose and solve the problem of artistic quality in a scientific way. This decisive question properly belongs to art criticism and the sociology of art.

The various criteria of judgment which general sociological and art historical studies might establish can, of course, be evaluated in their turn by rating the criterion of precious materials, for example, "lower" than that of "moral edification." But it should be remembered that "moral edification" led to the *bondieuserie* of St. Sulpice, whereas, without the criterion of precious materials, neither the hour-books of the Duc de Berry nor that of Étienne Chevalier would perhaps have ever been created. Or another example: for a sociologist it is not difficult to show why Manet was less liked by the general public and the official art establishment of the time than Meissonier or Bouguereau. But this explanation says nothing about the artistic quality of those painters. Is Meissonier "better" than Manet? Manet "better" than Meissonier? Are they of equal value? Similarly, a historian of civilization or a sociologist of knowledge can easily explain why Jacob Burckhardt placed Raphael far above Michelangelo, Corregio, and Rembrandt. While this is of great importance with regards to Jacob Burckhardt the humanist and his conception of the function of art, it says very little about the artistic value of the four masters. Finally, Diderot's enthusiastic praise of Greuze and his devastating criticism of Boucher are well known. Do the works of the two artists justify these different evaluations?

To put this in another way: the question of possible objective criteria of artistic quality must be distinguished from the question why the general public of Manet's time and Diderot and Jacob Burckhardt expressed the judgments they did. Rather, the question is: what is the scope of validity possessed by the statements on the relationship between man and man, between man and nature, the unity or dualism of reason and feeling, matter and mind, etc., which are transmitted, that is, expressed, by the objectively visible form-relationships of the work? If the potential content could be proved, in fact, to be the result of the form-relationships, it follows that it then must be equally possible to show that—and why—Rembrandt's late works are "greater" than the works of his early and middle periods, that Picasso is "better" than Dali, that Rubens' "Allegory of War" (Pitti Palace) is "greater" than Otto Dix' "War" but not "better," although more "beautiful" than Picasso's "Guernica."

After some detours the same point which was already stressed at the end of the description of the "Coronation of the Virgin" crops up again, namely: the importance of the expressive content as an objective, visible datum.

Up to now, however, the main point made was that the viewers' basic attitude, oriented either toward meaning or expression, decisively influences the judgment passed on every work of art, so that the evaluation of the expression may be dependent upon the meaning. But does not, perhaps, the expression, the potential content, nevertheless precede or influence the meaning? And if the meaning can indeed be influenced by the expression, how is it possible then that, in the course of time, ever so many different interpretations, of meaning and expression alike, are brought to bear upon a work which, in its visibility, remains the same? Has the quality of the work something to do with the possibility of such a multiplicity? Can the meaning fundamentally change the expression? To some degree only? Or, perhaps, not at all? Is the expression not necessarily predominant? And is the evaluation of the expression and the meaning of a work by its contemporaries necessarily "more correct" than that of posterity? Why and by what justification is then the "distance in time" always cited as the only criterion supposedly capable of proving the quality of a work of art?

Before attempting to answer these questions, which all spring from the problem of the "timeless" and "time-bound" character of the work of art, through detailed descriptive analyses of several very different works the "Coronation of the Virgin" can serve once more to show that the visual form-relationships do indeed determine the potential content. Nothing proves this point better than the contract which Jean de Montagnac, who commissioned the work, concluded in 1453 with Enguerrand Quarton, the painter responsible for the altarpiece to be executed.

Contract for an altarpiece to be painted for Dominus Jean de Montanac, priest.

Here follows the list of items of the altarpiece . . .

First: There should be the form of Paradise, and in that Paradise should be the Holy Trinity, and there should not be any difference between the Father and the Son; and the Holy Ghost in the form of a dove; and Our Lady in front as it will seem best to Master Enguerrand; and the Holy Trinity will place the crown on the head of Our Lady.

Item: The vestments should be very rich; those of Our Lady should be white-figured damask according to the judgment of said Master Enguerrand; and surrounding the Holy Trinity should be cherubim and seraphim.

Item: At the side of Our Lady should be the Angel Gabriel with a certain number of angels, and on the other side, Saint Michael, also with a certain number of angels, as it will seem best to Master Enguerrand.

Item: On the other side, St. John the Baptist with other patriarchs and prophets according to the judgment of Master Enguerrand.

Item: On the right side should be St. Peter and St. Paul with a certain number of other apostles.

Item: Beside St. Peter should be a martyr pope, over whose head an angel holds a tiara, together with St. Stephen and St. Lawrence in the habits of cardinal deacons, also with other martyr saints as arranged by the said Master.

Item: At the side of John the Baptist will be the Confessors. St. Gregory is to be recognized in the form of a pope as above, and two cardinals, one old and one young, and St. Agricola and St. Hugh Bishop (Saint Hugh in the habit of a Carthusian) and other saints according to the judgment of said Master Enguerrand.

Item: On the side of St. John the Baptist, Magdelene, and the two Marys, Jacob, and Salome, each of which holds in her hands that which they should hold, together with other widows according to the judgment of said Master Enguerrand.

Item: In Paradise below should be all the estates of the world arranged by said Master Enguerrand.

Item: Below the said Paradise, there should be the heavens in which will be the sun and the moon according to the judgment of said Master Enguerrand.

Item: After the heavens, the world in which should be shown a part of the city of Rome.

Item: On the side of the setting sun should be the form of the church of St. Peter of Rome, and, before said Church at an exit, one cone of pine in copper, and from there one descends a large stairway to the large square leading to the bridge of Sant'Angelo.

Item: At the left side of the above-mentioned, a part of the walls of Rome, and on the other side are houses and shops of all types; at the end of said square is the castle Sant' Angelo and a bridge over the Tiber which goes into the city of Rome.

Item: In said city are many churches, among these is the church of the Holy Cross of Jerusalem where Saint Gregory celebrated mass and there appeared to him Our Lord in the form of Pitie; in which church will be painted the story according to the arrangement of said Master Enguerrand; in that story will be Saint Hugh, the Carthusian, assisting said Saint Gregory with other prelates according to the judgment of said Master Enguerrand.

Item: Outside Rome, the Tiber will be shown entering the sea, and on the sea will be a certain number of galleys and ships.

Item: On the other side of the sea, will be a part of Jerusalem; first, the Mount of Olives where will be the cross of Our Lord, and at the front of this will be a praying Carthusian, and at a little distance will be the tomb of My Lord and an angel below saying: He has risen . . .[7]

Item: At the foot of said tomb will be two praying figures; on the right side, the valley of Jehoshaphet between the mountains, in that valley, a church where the tomb of Our Lady is, and an angel saying: Mary has been taken up to a heavenly chamber . . . and at the foot of that tomb a person praying.

Item: On the left side will be a valley in which will be three persons all of one age, from all three will come rays of sun, and there will be Abraham coming forth from his tabernacle and adoring the said three persons saying: Lord, if I have found favor . . .

Item: On the second mountain will be Moses with his sheep and a young boy carrying a bag; and there appears to said Moses, Our Lord in the form of a fire in the middle of a bush and Our Lord will say: Moses, Moses . . .

Item: On the right part will be Purgatory where the angels lead those joyously on seeing that they will go to Paradise from those the devils lead in great sadness.

Item: On the left side will be Hell, and between Purgatory and Hell will be a mountain, and from the part of Purgatory below the mountain will be an angel comforting the souls of Purgatory; and from the part of Hell will be a very disfigured devil turning his back to the angel and throwing certain souls into Hell, given him by other devils.

Item: In Purgatory and Hell will be all estates according to the judgment of said Master Enguerrand.[8]

The contract, whose preamble and conclusion have been omitted here, has been quoted in such detail because it so clearly demonstrates the emphasis on the meaning of the work.[9] It also becomes

7. The full text of scriptural passages prescribed to the painter has been omitted here.

8. English translation of the contract from Elizabeth G. Holt, *A Documentary History of Art*, vol. I (Doubleday Anchor, 1947) p. 298.

9. The fact that colors and forms were prescribed for the painter along with the characterization of figures as Carthusians, holy widows,

clear, however, that the earlier given sketch of the expressive content distinctly brought forth the *general* basic attitude of the painting without requiring prior knowledge of the meaning of all these details. But it follows precisely from the relatively unambiguous character of the potential content that the work will and must be evaluated quite differently in different periods, independently, to repeat, of its known meaning. An educated viewer living around the end of the eighteenth century, for example, might have rejected the work as "bad," not because he was an atheist or a deist, and not because he did not clearly understand the meaning of the representation, but rather because the arrangement of the whole, for example, could not be rationally understood. He need not have been aware of this at all; consciously he might only have been aware of the fact that he found the perspective wrong, the costumes "old-fashioned" or anachronistic, the gestures "stiff" or "inelegant." (All of which need not have kept him from thinking the colors "beautiful," or the little figures amusing or interesting.) In other words, what the imaginary eighteenth-century beholder would have rejected are the extra-artistic structural relationships which appear as form-relationships in the expressive content of the picture and which would have struck him as an already superseded stage of social development or a stage that needed to be superseded. A religious painting by Poussin, in contradistinction, might have been thoroughly satisfying to the same viewer.

That changing value judgments on works of art are a necessary result of the effect exercised by the potential content can be understood, however, only if it is possible to show that—and how—the form-relationships are molded by the historical situation in which the work of art was created and if this can be done without prior knowledge of that situation being a point of departure.

What happens when an analysis fails to consider the form-relationships and, instead, uncritically accepts the subject matter (the theme) of the work as the sole transmitter of expression can be illustrated by the following amusing examples whose absurd results, how-

---

cardinals, etc., will not be gone into here: the widows' headdresses are different from those of unmarried women, Carthusians wear *white* cowls, cardinals specific vestments, etc. Nor will the other aspects on which the contract sheds light—the role of the artist, the relation of the artist to the patron, etc.—be considered here.

ever, are kindred to many of today's "sociological" misinterpretations.[10]

"There can be no doubt that the most prominent features of the French at the beginning of the twentieth century were peace, calm, the quiet joys of the home and family life.... To judge from the testimony of the greatest masters, the normal way of life in France was very simple and had a picturesque charm vanished today. In the genre paintings of that period the most usual means of transportation is the gondola, the most widespread type of building the bower, and the tree most frequently encountered the cypress. Serenely and gravely, life was passed in shadowy parks, around splendid fountains, in elegant leisure."... This could very well be written one day, for none of our agitations, our tragedies, our crowds, and our labor entered into the works exhibited in that year [1914].

*Or:* Imagine the Grand Palais buried like Knossos or Susa, and after a thousand years a young archaeologist, on the site where Paris had been, uncovers the "Salon" intact. What a find! What perfect knowledge of the civilization of 1932. Society—so the archaeologist would write—consisted of generals, prelates, and Breton peasants. "It had been assumed that the décolleté garments called ballgowns were worn only in the evening. That is entirely inaccurate. We have a great number of pictures in which women, adorned with their jewelry, their shoulders bare, are obviously illuminated by daylight. But normally the women wore no clothing whatsoever, which indicates that they lived in a condition of servitude and subordination, which the literature of the period did not reveal. An intriguing mystery still envelops what was called 'the working classes.' Probably religious prohibitions stemming from a primitive taboo forbade the representation of work and ordinary life."

In the following descriptive analyses of three paintings, all of

10. Both examples are cited in Charles Lalo, *L'Expression de la Vie dans l'Art* (Paris: Alcan, 1933) pp. 176, 178.

which treat the same theme, social concepts will not be brought to bear on the works from the outside. Thus, investigation of the social, religious, etc., conditions in Giotto's, Bruegel's and Rubens' times does *not* constitute the point of departure, nor will the iconographical meaning of the pictures be considered. Instead, it will be shown that the expressive content of the three works rests on objective form-relationships which, in turn, give indications as to the historical (extra-artistic) conditions in their period of origin. The results of the analyses will show whether—and to what extent—this way of viewing paintings, which considers the historical conditions as immanent to the potential content, can help to answer the question concerning the possibility of objective judgments on artistic quality. Or whether it can at least make the answer possible *in principle*.

# 3.

# Giotto: "The Massacre of the Innocents"

Even the viewer who does not actually analyze Giotto's "Massacre of the Innocents" (fig. 4) will quickly gain the impression that in this work an event is related in such a way as to leave no doubt about its origin, its course, and its results. Whatever can be seen—every line, every directional emphasis, every figure or group of figures, every gesture—serves the rational elucidation of the occurrence. Indeed, the various elements that effect this rational clarity are to such a degree intertwined and functionally (spatially, descriptively, expressively) connected with each other that to change or omit a single element would destroy not only the artistic-logical unity of the picture (as happens in every good work of art) but its special rational-logical unity as well. In this work artistic logic and rational logic are indivisible.

The massacre must have been going on for quite a while. A heap of children's corpses, brutally flung to the ground, lies as a heavy horizontal mass in the foreground of the picture. This pile of bodies (each body distinctly displays a wound, so that any thought of a natural death becomes impossible) is bound on the left by the figure of a spectator, half turned away, half staring in fascinated horror. In spatial depth, the pile extends to the two henchmen in full activity, whereas on the right the hem of the dress of one of the mothers, who confront the executioners as a compact group, barely touches the slaughtered bodies. In its width the mass of corpses corresponds almost exactly to that of the murderers. Murderers and murdered ones are—as verticals and horizontals—clearly separated and yet very closely linked. They belong together.

But the slaughter continues. The ruler on the balcony high above all other figures, separated from them not only physically by the raised location[1] but furthermore emphatically set apart by the balustrade and the arch of the balcony, commandingly stretches his right

1. The balcony begins exactly above the picture's central horizontal and ends only at the upper edge of the picture.

4. *The Massacre of the Innocents* by Giotto
[Fotographie Anderson, Rome]

arm downward. There the command given by this gesture is carried out. The causal relation between the order for the massacre and its execution is unequivocally clear, for the diagonal of the arm[2] inevitably leads the eye to the executioners and their victims as well as to the lamenting, pleading, and resisting mothers of the victims.

No matter with which individual figure or group of figures the viewer begins and regardless of the varied way the connections between the executioners, the children, and the women are given, his eye is always led back from the victims to the author of the event.

At least some of these multiple connections (see fig. 5) shall be indicated here. The direction indicated by the outstretched arm leads across the distance that separates the ruler from the women, directly to the left hand, raised in defense, of the mother whose right hand still clings to the foot of the child that the hooded executioner is tearing away from her. This executioner stands directly under the vertical of the corner of the balcony,[3] which is intersected by the wrist of the ruler in such a way that his hand appears in complete isolation coloristically as well. Thus its particular significance is emphatically underlined. (If the hand were removed, the ruler would become a mere spectator, rather than the author, of the massacre!) In their opposite movements the two hands—the ruler's pointing downward, commanding, and that of the helpless mother raised in defense—correspond to each other on the same diagonal. In its continuation this diagonal cuts through the lower part of the body of the terrified child whom the woman in the right foreground is clasping passionately to her breast while the bearded executioner who stands almost in the center has already seized the child's left leg and raises his dagger to deliver the death blow. Finally, the same diagonal also traverses the figure of the third executioner, seen from the rear, in the lower right corner of the picture.[4] Thus this main directional thrust encompasses all the essential protagonists of the drama: the author, the agents, and the victims. The only figures who are not touched by this general compo-

2. It coincides in part exactly with the picture's diagonal which runs from the upper left to the lower right.

3. Thus the personage ordering the murder, the murderers, and the murdered victims on the ground are directly connected.

4. It cuts through his left leg at the bend of the knee and ends in his right foot.

5. Detail from *The Massacre of the Innocents* by Giotto [Fotographie Anderson, Rome]

sitional direction, who remain "outside," are the three spectators in the lower left corner of the picture, who do not act directly but merely react to what they behold.

The nexus between the figure giving the order and the consequences ensuing from his order is emphasized at every point in the work. It is impossible, for example, to overlook within the general direction of movement the child's arm, brutally grasped by the executioner under the balcony, which in its upward curve points back to the ruler's ominous hand. This raised child's arm,[5] however, leads the eye not only upwards and back to the ruler, but at the same time downward to the left, to the executioner who has seized it.[6] Thus the movement of the arm is clearly an accusatory expression and a representation of physical suffering.

For the eye, the arm is also inseparably linked with the countercurve which begins in the right hand and shoulder of the bearded executioner and in its uninterrupted broadening movement leads through his left arm, by way of the child clasped tightly by his mother on the right, over another child's head to the head of the last mother. Almost completely hidden by the third executioner, her head forms the end point of the whole compact group of women.[7]

5. The only form in the lower half of the picture that rises freely *above* its horizontal axis.

6. The curve of the child's arm is the direct continuation of the curve of the executioner's arm enveloped in folds. An imaginary line drawn from the child's hand over the hood, shoulder, and arm of the executioner and back through the child's chin and arm to the starting point, results in an approximate oval, i.e., a form which always reverts to itself. A larger oval—upright rather than horizontal—connects the child, the executioner, and the ruler if the curve of the child's arm is continued upward to the left arm of the ruler, and closes the oval by prolonging it from there downward through the ruler's right shoulder, the jutting corner of the balcony, and the executioner's arm.

7. The head of this woman not only forms the end point of the group of mothers but also the apex of an oval, actually several ovals, which are scarcely concealed as geometrical forms. A first oval isolates the women as a group in the solidarity of their unhappiness: the crucial line runs from the last woman's head down to the left through the arm of the child clinging to his mother. It is continued in the outstretched arm and hand of the mother vainly fighting for her child against the executioner, and then moves to the right, traversing the crossed, imploring hands of the tallest standing woman and then through the outline of *all* the women's heads back to the starting point. The second and third ovals, on the other hand, indicate again

Thus the fate of the one child is compositionally connected with that of the others and, without losing its significance as a single destiny, becomes an expressive part and conveyor of a collective fate.

But actually the children are not at all the key figures in this "Massacre of the Innocents," and neither the representation of their physical torment nor of their fear constitutes the essential expressive content of the work. Rather, what the picture as a whole and in every detail shows are the various types of human response in the face of arbitrary human violence and cruelty.

Three fundamental comportments correspond to the clearly differentiated main groups of the total composition. The largest and formally most coherent group is that of the women. Their compact mass is not very articulated and, in contrast to the group of spectators at the extreme left of the picture which consists of three figures only, the group as a whole by no means has the plastic weight of the figures of the executioners.[8] Nevertheless, the group of mothers (with the octagonal building behind them) not only balances the left half of the picture compositionally, but the mothers alone stand unitedly in the truest sense of the word "over against" the ruler and his henchmen. No doubt they are powerless, overcome by sheer physical force, as shown by the vain resistance two of the women oppose to the executioners. Yet it is also obvious that the resistance of these women is not only an individual act. They represent the response of the hardly distinguishable anonymous group of women in its entirety.

At the greatest distance from the women, in closest proximity to the two grim executioners and not far away, either, from the ruler stands that group which is the most psychologically differentiated and complicated one, namely the spectators. Their place in the com-

---

the reason for the sorrow that overcomes all the women: the lower curve of the ovals, which lie in the same direction, includes either only the executioner standing closest to the women and his victim, or the hooded executioner as well. In the first case the lower curve traverses the body and leg of the only child that is entirely visible, upward through the raised right arm of the executioner, and back through the elbow of the oft-mentioned raised child's arm and the outline of the women's heads. In the second case —the larger of the two ovals—the executioner's hood becomes the left apex of the oval.

8. Every reader can easily check this by closing his eyes for a minute and asking himself which figures persist more clearly in his memory, individual women or individual executioners.

position already characterizes their inner attitude, so essentially different from that of the women and the executioners. For in their actual, spatial location the spectators stand "on the side" of the author of the massacre and the murderers accomplishing the deed.[9] Their gestures, their postures, and their faces express—each in a different way—disgust, horror, sympathy. In other words, whereas in the ruler, executioners, and women, psychological attitude and physical action form a unity, the spectators manifest a conflict between will and action, or better, exhibit an ambiguous attitude. This ambiguity is immediately revealed externally in the contrast between their spatial location and their physiognomic reactions and, above all, in the contrast between their emotional involvement and their actual passivity. This twofold contrast characterizes each of the three spectators.[10] That the spectators' lack of activity is the consequence of an inner indecision is made all the clearer by the fact that the gestures and actions of all the other figures are always concretely motivated.[11] Such external, that is, *visible* rational motivation is entirely lacking in the spectators—they are not, for example, inferior to the executioners in numbers, they are not threatened by any visible opponent, and they are not portrayed as being physically weak.

Externally free, the reason for the passivity of the spectators therefore can lie only in themselves. Thus the group of spectators with-

9. In other ways, too, they are more closely formally connected with them than with the other figures: the verticals of the middle and left columns of the balcony are continued in the two figures standing directly in front of and under them and, as such, they form parallels to the hooded executioner. In terms of space and mass the large frontal figure of the group corresponds to the executioner seen from the back. But in terms of expression the executioner blocks any way out for the women, whereas the spectator in the foreground seems to want to leave the scene of the drama.

10. Thus the monumental figure in the foreground, shown in its full width, forms the greatest contrast in terms of direction to the two executioners, and the man with his head lowered slightly is probably looking at the corpses at his feet with horror or pained sympathy. But he does nothing. Similarly, the man standing behind the executioner is turning his head away because he cannot bear, or does not want to see, the gruesome sight before him, but he too remains passive. The figure at the extreme edge of the painting, already cut off by the frame, is again turned toward the massacre, with a facial expression that is hard to define. But like his two companions he too does nothing.

11. For example, the gesture of the ruler giving the order for the massacre, the physical strength of the executioners and their methodical actions, the helplessness of the women and their various gestures, etc.

in the picture becomes the prototype of everyone who looks at it. For the real viewer also is a "spectator" of the event with which Giotto confronts him as an objective, self-sufficient reality. Precisely through this objectivity the picture addresses every beholder with the very question so contradictorily answered by the spectators in the picture: the question of one's personal position in the face of arbitrary violence and human suffering.

To sum up the form-relationships underlying the expressive content of the work: the total structure of the picture is determined by a unitary rational conception unfailingly preserved throughout the work. The event portrayed is comprehensible in terms of its own internal system of reference, that is, it appears to the viewer as an autonomous, objective reality. There are no independent details in the picture. Indeed, each individual form (a line, a hand, a fold in a garment) fulfills a function (spatial, objective-explicatory, coloristic, etc.) as an element in the optical unity of the picture. But whatever the particular functions—and one form always fulfills several functions—all these individual forms possess expressive value only within the totality of the picture.

All the personages in the picture are presented as being fundamentally of equal value and essentially alike. Their different importance in the event is not characterized by differences in size, individual physiognomy, and so forth, but by their importance as actors. They appear as representatives of group communities, as types. The basic spiritual response shown in each of these types (imploring, murdering, hesitating) is always depicted in several figures, and varied each time through different postures and gestures.

The ruler, the *spiritus rector* of all the actions and reactions, in contradistinction to all the other figures, alone is represented in emphatic isolation.

Bodies and architectures appear as solid, articulated masses; their particular textures (stone, skin, hair), however, are distinguished only to the extent absolutely necessary for comprehension. The texture as such is not emphasized as a value.

Giotto's much discussed representation of space shows all objects as convincing volumes, but no space constructed independently of the bodies (objects) exists. Only physical being has spatial reality; and the unified picture space is not an abstract-conceptual entity logically and artistically prior to the being of the volumes. Rather, this picture-space results from the positioning of the bodies or the distances between them.

Now, do these results permit conclusions regarding the general extra-artistic structural relationships or the philosophical presuppositions within the framework of which the work was created? And to what extent on this basis can Giotto's fresco be considered as an "expression of his time?"

A first although quite general characterization of the audience[12] to which the work addressed itself springs from its theme and the location for which it was commissioned. For since the "Massacre of the Innocents" belongs to a cycle of representations from the lives of Christ and Mary adorning the walls of a church, the work presumes a community unified, at least, by the institutional form of a religious faith and thereby places the work and the community within the context of a certain tradition. But this overly broad presupposition with respect to the origination of the work cannot explain either the specific form of the picture, nor does it permit conclusions as to the specific character of the religious community. For, after all, the Church as an institution and the tradition of monumental ecclesiastical art have a history preceding Giotto by more than a thousand years.

The fact, however, that the subject matter of the religious story is presented as a sequence of causes and effects graspable by the standards of human insight, human intellect, and human feeling (whereby the content of the religious story remains intact), the fact that the picture is potentially "self-explanatory," is historically unthinkable without positing a particular type of audience. These viewers must in principle at least be ready and able to accept situations, actions, events, and things as objective data whose aspects, interconnections or possibilities can be understood by human experience and human reflection, independently of transcendental presuppositions. In this context, too, it remains true that without Giotto "Jan Steen would have been different (and presumably less great)."[13]

In short, in a general way the rationality of the pictorial

12. For the indissoluble connection between the work of art and the public see Chapter 7.

13. True, in this passage Burckhardt is *not* speaking of the "new" in Giotto but rather emphasizing the importance of "hieratic" styles.

structure points to a certain rationality in the mental attitude of the viewer. But that is not saying very much unless it is possible to define this attitude more exactly and to do so on the basis of the particular manner that determines the autonomous character and the inner laws of the pictorial reality. For the particularity of the pictorial structure consists precisely in the fact that the diverse elements of the picture are used as vehicles of interconnected functions all of which serve one purpose, namely to make the essential features of the story visible with the utmost clarity. Thus the pictorial structure fully corresponds to that "spirit," or that mentality which authors of diverse persuasions have called variously "market-oriented rationality" (Max Weber), "substantial" rationality (Karl Mannheim), or the "merchant's mentality" (A. von Martin). No matter how far apart these authors may be in terms of methods, they all are in agreement in one respect, namely, in seeing this mentality, "new" when compared to that of the Middle Ages, as the consequence of a change in social and economic structure whose origins are traceable to the twelfth century, but whose most distinctive and earliest manifestation occurred in Florence in the thirteenth and fourteenth centuries—the rise of early capitalism and the development of an economically and politically independent middle class.

Of course neither the various stages of this development can be pursued here nor can its economic, social, and political results be described in detail. The only point to be made at this moment is that the relation existing between the new structure of Giotto's picture and the new early capitalist social structure of his time is not direct; rather it is mediated by the new mentality, the new rationalism. This mediation takes place in such a way that the new mental attitude appears as a *presupposition* of the pictorial structure whereas this very presupposition is the *end result* of the extra-artistic structural changes which took place in the course of the historical development in manifold interactions and overlaps.

However, in Giotto's work this "new spirit" does not remain a mere "presupposition" but is artistically molded to perfection. And it is precisely for this reason that elements which correspond and point to the extra-artistic, historical origination of this new spirit, penetrate his artistic creation. And on the other hand, precisely because this new mentality was fully absorbed by the work and appears in purely artistic form, Giotto's genius corresponded to the artistic needs of the "most advanced" public of his time. More exactly, the pictorial structure of his work refers to certain social groups because only the new dominant upper strata could develop, by virtue of their special position of material, political, and social power, that "objective distance" to things and to "reality" with which Giotto, in Dvorak's words, objectively confronts the "real world" with an "autonomous work of art."[14]

This new mentality, the end result of a long and complex development, can be approximately described in a schematic and oversimplified way: the early capitalist market economy and its mode of production are characterized by a gradual rationalization of labor. The object produced for the market, the commodity, is the result of an increasingly manifold division of labor (Weber's "Leistungsspezialisierung," specialization of achievement), whose separate activities are functionally interconnected. The rational purposiveness of this division of labor, however, cannot be understood from the standpoint of the worker specialized for the performance of a partial task only, but solely from the standpoint of the entrepreneur or contractor who determines the process as a whole and channels it for his gain without participating therein otherwise than financially and administratively. Hence the entrepreneur, as a result of his necessarily broader vision and, in consequence, greater differentiation of his innate abilities, develops a more encompassing objective and essentially rationally oriented mentality. Giotto's pictorial structure and the specific way each figure or form fulfills different functions all of which serve a *single* goal can by no means therefore be considered as an "expression of his time" in general but only as the expression of a dominant stratum of his contemporary society.[15]

14. See especially *Geschichte der italienischen Kunst im Zeitalter der Renaissance*, vol. I (Munich: 1927) pp. 16, 18, 20, 21, 43. Also *Ueber Greco und den Manierismus, Kunstgeschichte als Geistesgeschichte* (Munich: 1924) pp. 127, 265.

15. Likewise, this increasing specialization ushered in by the Renaissance provides one of the reasons which explains the separation of the fine arts into an art only for the "cultured" and an art for the "uneducated," a division which also originated in the Renaissance. (Focillon already emphasized that the *uomo universale* belongs—not as an ideal but as reality—to the Middle Ages and not to the Renaissance.) It is to be hoped that one day the entire problem of an "art for the educated" will be

But though this mentality has clearly and unmistakably penetrated Giotto's work as a presupposition and has been transmuted into visible form, at the same time the picture goes far beyond this historically determined presupposition. For this reason any attempt to read concrete historical details directly out of Giotto's work—for example, the relationship between the tiny Florentine elite and the mass of politically powerless and economically wretched people in the lower strata—is doomed to failure. Indeed, any viewer starting out solely from Giotto's representation of the "Massacre of the Innocents" (or any other work by Giotto), independently of all historical knowledge, would be led to a conclusion that directly contradicts historical reality, namely, the impression of a harmonious society in which every individual is an equal and essentially kindred member of a group in which all human relations (actions and feelings) not only are intelligible to human reason but also appear to be the result of a fundamentally rational order.

This equality shared, in principle, by all men is not impaired by the fact that in the "Massacre of the Innocents" the author of the whole event, the ruler, is isolated from all the groups affected by his command.[16] For even though the isolation expresses in visual terms the special causal importance of the figure, the figure itself is not essentially different from those who react to his action. In other words, the expressed difference in importance of the people always appears as the (logical) consequence of their actions, and the possibility of action is, in principle, the same for all men.

Thus Giotto's work presents as reality that which in actual fact did not exist at the stage of development reached at this time, namely, a society where men's common experience manifests itself in

---

thoroughly researched. Such a project would form a necessary complement to the studies of specific problems so brilliantly pursued, above all, by the scholars of the Warburg Institute.

16. This isolation of the figure responsible for the action from all the others occurs in all of Giotto's works, though rarely in such pronounced confrontation as in the "Massacre of the Innocents"; most frequently it takes the form of a rhythmic isolation. See, for example, the isolation of Christ in the "Raising of Lazarus," the isolation of Mary in the fresco of the "Wedding Procession," (both in Padua) or the figure of the miracle-working St. John in the "Raising of Drusiana" in Santa Croce, Florence.

social relationships from which no one is excluded and which can be understood by all. And yet, this statement in no wise contradicts the previous reflections. For the creation of such a society is contained in the new rationalism of Florentine early capitalism, as a necessary (although not necessarily conscious) theoretical possibility and goal. Since this rationalism was preserved as the fundamental formative principle in Giotto's work, to the extent that—and because—his art transcends the social reality of his time, his work is not a sentimentalized, dishonest, or "realistic" reflection of this historical reality but its genuine ideal image. In other words, Giotto's pictorial world anticipates the fulfillment of possibilities latent in the historical reality of his time but which, in fact, were developed only one-sidedly and imperfectly.[17] Whether this genuine transcendence of historically conditioned reality, as in classic Greek art, gives Giotto's art its dimension of "timelessness" will be discussed in Chapter 6.

17. The fact that in the universe and humanity created by Giotto the basic unity of the external world appears mightier than its various manifestations is probably to be understood also as the transcendence of historical reality rather than as the heritage of medieval world views. Inasmuch as Giotto's work is thoroughly anchored in tradition and continues it, in terms of its religious meaning, the rational unity of his work (*and* the plastic intensity of his figures) objectively visible in it nevertheless stands in contrast to the profusion of realistic details characteristic of the "typically" medieval representations (or the typical *later* style of "International Gothic"). This realistic richness of detail fully corresponds to the oft-cited passage from Thomas of Aquinas that "God rejoices in all things because each of them actually coincides with His essence." But it does not follow therefrom that the unity of all things in God must—or can—be rendered objectively in works of art. Rather, in contrast to Giotto's work, this unity is *posited* as being subjectively known or felt by the beholder. This is confirmed even by the highest attainable objectification of this unity, the Gothic cathedral. See the admirable study by Otto von Simson, *The Gothic Cathedral*, Bollingen Series XLVIII (New York: Pantheon, 1956).

# 4.

# Bruegel: "The Massacre of the Innocents"

A troop of fully armored soldiers has ridden into a snow-covered village whose street, a squared extension of which leads directly to the viewer (fig. 6), is framed irregularly by gabled houses and bare trees. The commander, clothed in black—the only one without arms—is easily recognizable in the front rank.

It is clear that the soldiers have ridden in from the background of the picture, where the street near the church bends between houses and leads over a narrow bridge, inasmuch as one of the soldiers has been left behind on the bridge as a guard. Thus the village is sealed off at the back and behind the soldiers the street is lifeless. Why, is indicated by what is happening in front of them.

Lances raised, without dismounting, the troop has halted at a point which is not only geometrically of "central importance,"[1] but which within the picture also corresponds to the objectively most suitable strategic point: the whole village is surveyable at a glance to the soldiers—and to the viewer of the picture as well.

Thus the mounted group and the beholder become counterparts, since all the events represented occur in the space between the soldiers and the beholder—the murder, pleas for mercy, excited discussions and lamentations, violent entry into houses, futile attempts to escape, and cold-blooded pursuit.

With a single exception the troop of knights is as little involved, actively and directly, in the event as is the viewer. Nevertheless their wedge-shaped, dark metal-colored group dominates the action as though it were the embodiment of a sinister fate which no

---

1. It lies exactly on the vertical central axis and directly above the horizontal central line of the picture.

6. *The Massacre of the Innocents* by Bruegel [Kunsthistorisches Museum, Wien]

one can escape. Nor is the viewer left in doubt about the fact that the order for the deeds stems from the armored men and their leader. For in the exact center of the picture (fig. 7), immediately in front of the rigid mass of horsemen and directly under the eyes of their chief, two or three dismounted men-in-arms and a few lansquenets form the upper part of a circle around some children being speared to death like animals at the end of a battue.[2] This is the only scene in the picture in which the armored riders are actively engaged in the slaughter—as though by this one example they wanted to show the mercenaries what to do and how to do it. Everywhere else the task of seizing the victims, murdering them, breaking into houses, and pursuing fugitives is left to subordinates—to red-jacketed horsemen and foot soldiers armed with swords.

But the armored horsemen are always supervising and guiding the execution of the orders. For instance, in the lower right corner of the picture near the willow stumps next to the frozen pond, one of them, his command staff outstretched, is ordering the forcing of a house door. Two subordinates, kicking, are carrying out the order with a pike and a log. In the left foreground two other armored men stop their horses alongside a group of two red-jacketed riders. And while one lance-bearer listens to a report or gives orders, his companion, motionless and aloof as a statue, observes the imminent stabbing of a child being wrested from an imploring woman.

But even where the knights are not intervening in the event at all, it is clear that they are the authors responsible for the actions depicted. For all the many figures and groups, which at first seem to be completely autonomous and (formally) independent, are, when seen within the picture as a whole, but components of larger entities, all of which depend on the central "fate-group." This dependence, however, is seldom explicit.

For example, the woman in the lower left corner (fig. 8), the red-jacketed rider brandishing a pike, and the dog running alongside the horse appear—when considered in isolation—to form a wholly independent group that needs no further explanation either in terms

2. The other half of the circle consists of the figures of the weeping and lamenting women precipitately fleeing in all directions from the murder site, to the right and left, backward and forward.

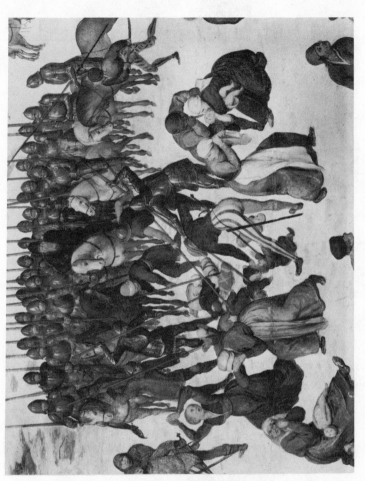

7. Detail from *The Massacre of the Innocents* by Bruegel [Kunsthistorisches Museum, Wien]

8. Detail from *The Massacre of the Innocents* by Bruegel [Kunsthistorisches Museum, Wien]

of form or expression. The flight and pursuit speak for themselves. Spatially, this woman is at the greatest distance from the metallic central group and nothing indicates that any of the armored horsemen is watching her in particular.

But *why* is the woman fleeing, holding her child? *Why* does the rider set out after her? *Why* the weapon in his hand? The answer lies in the main structural lines of the picture. Those lines link the fleeing woman compositionally not only with all the other figures that seem equally independent and autonomous, but like them and through them she is causally linked with the "fate-group": an uninterrupted sequence of single figures and groups (their arrangement produces a slightly crooked line) leads the eye from the woman and the rider in the lower left to the armed men in the center. The line touches the soldier with drawn dagger running up to the fleeing woman from the right (thus the rider is not the only pursuer); the woman who wrings her hands, moaning over a child lying dead on the ground (children have been killed); the small group composed of a man, a woman, a soldier, and two children (children are being murdered everywhere); and the group of peasants huddled closely together in an excited and troubled discussion (general unrest and confusion prevails). Finally, the line ends in the wall-like mass of men-in-arms.

It is important to emphasize the particular nature of this compositional method, which seems to preserve, indeed to emphasize, •the autonomy of all parts of the picture while negating them at the same time. Each figure and each detail (the soldier running, the bare trees, the lamenting woman, the village pond) appears as a world in itself—the famous "pictures from Bruegel's pictures."[3] Thus, at first the whole picture gives the impression of a motley crowd, of a hustle and bustle which seems to be entirely "accidental," "haphazard," "natural." The actual structure underlying the multitude (and without which the painting would appear as confused and unintelligible as a snapshot of a real mass scene) remains hidden, above all because the coloristic composition of the picture does *not* coincide with it. Red, blue, and yellow, for example, permeate the whole painting and are

3. Gustav Glueck, *Bilder aus Bruegels Bildern* (Vienna: Schroll und Co., 1936). How impossible it would be, in contrast, to isolate "pictures from Giotto's pictures"!

repeated as local colors in the various figures and objects. But even if the eye follows these accents, spread over the whole picture—such as the use of red for the three riders in the left foreground—they do not constitute a specific visual path. On the contrary, the colors underline, in the truest sense of the word, the impression of an accidental "motley crowd"; and although by their repetitions they contribute to the optical unity of the picture as a whole and bind the multiple elements together, they emphasize just as strongly the separateness of each particular scene or particular form.

Indeed it is precisely the hidden, indirect compositional lines that tie the different "worlds" of the particular scenes, the "microcosms," together causally and in terms of subject matter and that show their manifold conditioned dependencies in the picture as a whole, the "macrocosm." Thus they relativize if not abolish the autonomy of these scenes. Inasmuch as this principle of the concealed direction of the compositional lines underlies the total pictorial structure, two further examples will be cited for its demonstration.

It is obvious that the figures of the woman and her pursuer mentioned above belong, spatially and coloristically, to the group of three riders to her right who stand turned toward the middle ground of the picture, at a right angle to the pursuer's horse. But two new directional lines of vision and movement start out from this group of riders, both of which connect the left foreground with the right half of the picture (middle ground and foreground), and which also connect in each case the superiors with their subordinates, the wrongdoer with the victims, and single figures with groups, in such a way that each visual path ends with those giving the orders and those executing them, or with those in command and their victims:[4] from the group of riders,

---

4. The first path of vision leads as a diagonal through the horse of the yellow-jacketed trumpeter and the torso of the red-jacketed man with the richly feathered hat next to him, to the aforementioned armored lance-bearers and from there traversing the woman in the red dress with the blue apron sitting flat on the snow, holding the naked corpse of her child in her lap, to the grief-stricken and hand-wringing women trying to get away from the slaughter in the picture's center. In an arc these fleeing figures guide the eye to the right, to the group of peasants, surrounding the horse of the "herald," (see note 8, p.47) and to the adjacent violent scene of a house being broken into. The first visual path ends in this scene. For the diagonal formed by the wall of the house, which leads both into the background and

encompassing those in command, the actual perpetrators, and their victims, to the two houses on the right being rammed which include commanders and perpetrators.

An arc composed of the many particular scenes, each of which reveals a different aspect of the individual and collective reactions to the event, stretches between the point of departure and these end points. In the left foreground, for example, a poor wretch kneeling humbly in the snow—beside him the cap which he has respectfully removed in the presence of authority, his arms imploringly raised—pleads with one of the red-jacketed riders who does not even give him a glance. This scene is thoroughly devoid of sentimentality, of pathos and heroism. But for precisely this reason it tragically underlines—for the *modern* viewer[5]—the contrast between spontaneous human feeling (the peasant's imploring gesture) and professional inhumanity (the indifference of the horseman).

Another example: the group of villagers, men and women, who are excitedly surrounding the horse of a man in a blue blouse and a red beret with a feather (right middle ground). Obviously they expect him to give advice or help. He, however, the authority in charge, without dismounting reacts only by making a half-defensive, half-embarrassed gesture while next to him soldiers are forcibly breaking into a

---

down to the lower right of the foreground, belongs to another structural line in terms of direction, spatially, and in its compositional function.

The second path of vision, which begins in the group of riders in the left foreground, delineates a flat arc. Its terminal points lie between the hind legs of the horses of the two red riders and to the right at the corner of the house whose door is being rammed and kicked in. More particularly, this arc goes through the red-jacketed man on the right and curves, barely touching the head of the white horse and the front leg of the dark horse of the two obliquely placed lance-bearers, over the heads of the double group with the soldier tearing a child away from its parents and that of the three lamenting peasants (all turned to the left); the highest points of the curve lie at the top of the soldier's head who is drawing his sword and on the man in the red cap who is restraining the dog (all facing right). Then the arc descends over the group (all facing left again) in which two soldiers wrest a child from its mother, and traverses the willow stump next to the lance-bearer, his horse and the two soldiers breaking into the house.

5. For a compilation of the changing interpretations of Bruegel, a subject to be discussed later, see, for example, Ed. Michel, *Gazette des Beaux-Arts*, vol. I (1938) p. 27 ff. and F. Grossmann, *The Paintings of Pieter Bruegel* (London: Phaidon, 1955) pp. 29–38.

house under the leadership of one of the red-jacketed riders who, like himself, is elevated above the peasants.

The gestures and postures of the aforementioned individual figures or groups all differ from one another;[6] actually no repetitions ever occur in all the profusion of the figures. Yet the many figures do not display any comparable wealth of emotions or of individually differentiated behavior. *One* basic mood dominates the expression of all the victims, just as the one group of armored men dominates the event. The gestures and facial expressions of the peasants show bewildered helplessness, the dull uncomprehending horror of people caught up by a natural catastrophe to which they are defenselessly delivered. This sort of helpless surrender to an incomprehensible happening is expressed with particular clarity in that none of the many peasants makes even a single gesture of active resistance. Only rarely is there even an attempt to move those in command, the murdering soldiers, by pleas or entreaties (as does the peasant kneeling in the foreground). There is no resistance, no salvation save through flight.[7]

The detached, impersonal attitude of those in command and the brutality of the soldiers contrasts sharply with the (individual and collective) resigned passivity of the victims. Whereas the armored lance-bearers and the red-jacketed riders are easily distinguishable from the villagers not only by their dress and weapons but also by the fact that they seem to be taller and more controlled in their bearing than the peasants, only the actions and weapons of the foot soldiers distinguish executioners from victims.[8]

6. Even the figures in the picture that bear most resemblance to each other are never identical. For example, the bent-over woman in the right foreground who distraughtly lifts her hands to her mouth, and the woman in the left foreground, likewise bent-over, who laments, her hands raised and joined, the dead child on the ground.

7. The painting shows still another vain attempt at flight by a woman with her child: a woman tries to escape from the yellow-brown corner house on the picture's right (middle ground). A soldier already lies in wait to seize her.

8. For example, is the man with the red cap (right foreground) who restrains a large village dog by its collar a peasant or a lansquenet? Only a careful analysis can exactly answer the question: it is a peasant. But neither can the rider in the right middle ground, surrounded by peasants, be immediately identified as a representative of those in power although he is distinguished from the peasants by his dress and the fact that he is mounted.

This basic similarity in physical type of peasants and soldiers further reinforces the impression of confusion and tumultuous to and fro that a sudden attack by an armed and organized power on a peaceful village inevitably engenders, and as perceived by the eye as it glides in all directions through the picture, from one scene to the other, back to front and front to back, constantly falling upon figures resembling each other and which now are victims, now agressors.

Without exception, each single figure is a direct participant in the event—as commander, actor or victim. Within the picture there are no onlookers. The only "onlooker" is *outside* the picture. His concrete existence is posited by the pictorial reality whose particular space implies his presence as a neutral observer, as a person that is, who surveys the action without being involved in it. Yet this observer is not comparable to a spectator in a theatre (or to the viewer of a picture by Giotto or Rubens), on the stage of which a self-contained action is being performed from which the spectator is necessarily excluded, no matter how much he may, in feeling or thoughts, "identify" with the characters. Though the village and the events in it are spread out in objective clarity before the eyes of the beholder, he does not see them as if from a world that is spatially independent and cut off from the pictorial reality. The viewer's slightly raised location is the *continuation of the pictorial space* (in contrast to the stage in the traditional theater or to Giotto's spatial stage) without, however, becoming a "real space" as is the case, for example, in the illusionistically painted ceilings of the Baroque period. The viewer of Bruegel's picture remains *within the pictorial space* even though—and precisely because—the strong centrifugal movement of the figures and the whole spatial movement of the painting lead beyond the frame toward him. None of the figures shown address themselves to the viewer by glance or gesture (as in many paintings of the early and high Baroque) in order to entangle him not only spatially but also physically, spiritually, or emotionally in the pictorial event. The autonomy and objectivity of the

---

At first glance he might be a village elder, raised above the mass of villagers but powerless against any higher officialdom whose authority extends beyond the village community. Only close observation reveals that he is wearing a coat of mail and that his upper garment is decorated with a heraldic eagle. Grossmann, *op. cit.*, p. *199*, calls him a "herald."

pictorial space are preserved, as are the viewer's autonomy and own reality.[9] In other words: the given pictorial space logically explains and is connected with the beholder's (subjective) location without his becoming a participant in the event depicted.

This is why the subjectivity of the painter and viewer appear as the objectivity of observation. The representation thus acquires the character of a "factual report" *sine ira et studio*: it becomes an objective portrayal of various episodes of an empirical reality, and every beholder is left free—or every beholder is forced—to interpret this reality in *his own way*. Therein, and not in the subject matter of the picture, lies one of the main reasons why Bruegel's work as a whole has produced in the course of time such extraordinarily contradictory interpretations and reactions—from the "comic" to the "pessimistic" Bruegel.

Thus, the specific characteristics and the particular expressive content of Bruegel's creative method become manifest by way of this contrast, namely, that the artist on the one hand strongly emphasizes the actual, empirical aspects of the event while on the other he de-emphasizes the link existing between the various facts and hints only indirectly at the possible causal relationships. A previously mentioned characteristic feature of the pictorial structure thereby now reveals its full importance for the work's expressive content: all the understated and barely indicated causal relationships or other compositional features which point to the central group of men-in-arms as the authors of the slaughter are recognizable as such only for an observer detached from the event. No indirect relationships exist for those participating in the actions whether as actors or victims. For those, each deed ensues directly from a particular action, unexplained and inexplicable as to its causes, and each fate remains a particular fate.

It is precisely this direct effect of the actions that the picture presents as an observed reality in each of the many figures. Inasmuch as the artist shows the total reality of the village world as being the sum of many particular destinies, this reality, the observed world, itself becomes just as inexplicable and incomprehensible as each individual

9. Exaggeratedly it could be said that in the relation between the reality of the picture and that of the beholder the reality of the picture is prior to that of the beholder, whereas in the Baroque or in the Middle Ages the reality, or the claim to reality of the picture, is grounded in the (subjective) conceptual world of the beholder, which determines feeling and faith.

fate. In other words, not reality but the meaning of reality is called into question in the picture.

For although the beholder is able to recognize the dependence of the individuals on the central "fate-group," this knowledge does not explain the reason for the event. On the contrary, the insight into the conditioned nature of the seemingly independent actions proves, rather, that the question concerning the "why" of it all is repeated in a more encompassing form without receiving an answer. The question of the reason for or the meaning of the event is also posed only indirectly just as are the structural interconnections in the picture. The picture shows merely that the world *is* this way.

Is there an explanation why the world is the way it is? Must the viewer give an answer? Can he find an answer? And would the answer be the same if the viewer were not a viewer but a participant in the event? The picture and the painter do not give us an answer to the question. The artist shows only the reality or, as Montaigne says, "he proposes facts to men."

I was just now musing, as I often do, on how free and vague an instrument human reason is. I see ordinarily that men, when facts are put before them, are more ready to amuse themselves by inquiring into their reason than by inquiring into their truth. They leave aside the cases and amuse themselves treating the causes. Comical prattlers!

The knowledge of causes belongs only to Him who has the guidance of things, not to us who have only the endurance of them, and who have the perfectly full use of them according to our nature, without penetrating to their origin and essence. Nor is wine pleasanter to the man who knows its primary properties. On the contrary, both the body and the soul disturb and alter the right they have to the enjoyment of the world by mixing into it the pretension to learning. Determining and knowing, like giving, appertains to rule and mastery; to inferiority, subjection, and apprenticeship appertains enjoyment and acceptance. Let us return to this habit of ours.

They pass over the facts, but they assiduously examine their consequences. They ordinarily begin thus: "How does this happen?" What they should say is: "But does it happen?" Our reason is capable of filling out a hundred other worlds and finding their principles and contexture. It needs neither matter nor basis; let it run on; it builds as well on emptiness as on fullness, and with inanity as with matter. . . .

Truth and falsehood are alike in face, similar in bearing, taste and movement: we look upon them with the same eye. . . . It is unfortunate to be in such a pass that the best touchstone of truth is the multitude of believers, in a crowd in which the fools so far surpass the wise in number. . . . It is a difficult thing to set one's judgment against accepted opinions.

. . . For my part, in a matter on which I would not believe one, I would not believe a hundred ones. And I do not judge opinions by their years.[10]

It would certainly be objectionable to try, on the basis of a single painting by Bruegel and a single quotation from Montaigne, to establish exact parallels between these two contemporaries. It is not, however, a matter of parallels but of the fundamental similarity between the attitude of the skeptical philosopher and the expressive content of the picture: Montaigne and the painting both call into question the sense of the historically given order of the world (or the intelligibility and mastery of the existing order with the aid of human reason) without thereby denying the reality of what exists; and Bruegel's particular creative method makes no less an urgent appeal to the individual viewer's critical faculty than the writer who expressly takes the situation of the individual (himself) as the point of departure for his observations and reflections.

Not that Bruegel depicts individuals. On the contrary, what characterizes Bruegel is that, despite the convincing lifelike quality of all his figures, his work (and not only picture under discussion) seldom shows figures that are psychologically individualized or portrait-like and that there are no actual main figures in his work; the

10. Michel de Montaigne, *Essays*, III, 11, "Of Cripples," *The Complete Works of Montaigne*, translated by Donald M. Frame (Stanford University Press, 1957) pp. 785 and 786.

"conveyor of the action" is never a single personality but always the crowd, the anonymous mass.

Although it is extremely important to emphasize that the mass as such becomes the main protagonist, it is no less important to stress once again that the pictorial structure decidedly sets the individual beholder over against this mass. And since, as has already been shown, every viewer must judge and evaluate the reality depicted according to his own criteria, Bruegel's picture reveals both the special significance and the problem-complex of the individual in his relationship to the world that environs him.

For a conception of the world which attributes to the individual the ability to judge the events of the world in his own terms necessarily posits a historical situation in which it is practically and theoretically possible to develop a personality which is to a far extent independent of exterior and internal restrictions. Similarly, a conception of the world which impels the individual to judge actuality on his own posits in turn a historical situation in which existing external or internal conditions, ties, laws, and principles fail to provide men with a satisfactory explanation of the world around them and of their own existence. Obviously in such a situation religious doctrine and the institutions which transmit it can no longer be universally binding.

In this context it is immaterial whether the loss of ecclesiastical (or religious) authority is considered to be cause or consequence of the development of the helpless or self-conscious individual or whether both phenomena are viewed as the outcome of entirely different (social, political, economic) developments. At all events the total secularization of the old Biblical theme in Bruegel's work attests that the unity of the religious world view has been destroyed.

The secular character of the picture, however, does not derive from the fact that the story is depicted as a contemporary event, but rather from the relentless objectivity of the representation, which has already been discussed—the sheer matter-of-factness with which the event is portrayed, oriented neither toward heaven nor hell.[11]

In short, it is the particular delineation of the relation between the beholder and the event represented (and *not* the subject mat-

11. Max Friedlander, *Von Eyck bis Bruegel*, second ed. (Berlin: 1921) p. 178.

ter of the picture) which, together with the marked empiricism of the representation, point to a world which is "out of joint."[12] Thus the expressive content is above all the expression of a general historical situation, a general *Zeitgeist*, and what the expressive content of the "Massacre of the Innocents" conveys is no more characteristic of the particular situation in the Dutch provinces shortly before the outbreak of the eighty-year war against Spain than it is of the *Zeitgeist* in France at the time of the Huguenot wars.

Naturally, the statement that conditions in the Netherlands and France in the last third of the 16th century were similar and conduced to similar results presupposes some historical information. But does the painting, as visual representation independent of such knowledge, provide an indication of these particular conditions?

It must first be noted that Bruegel's representation of a "contemporary event"[13] by no means can be related to any specific occurence, even iconographically. For although the scenes in the "Massacre of the Innocents" are doubtlessly based on actual visual observations, the representation remains historically ambiguous. It can be interpreted with equal justification as the forcible collection of taxes or as a proceeding of the Inquisition, as the punitive action of a city, a feudal lord, or a bishop against a refractory rural populace or as the persecution of religious sectarians.

12. This does not mean, of course, that every contemporary viewer was aware of this fact nor necessarily felt it to be tragic. This assumption would be all the more unjustified, because the individual contemplating and judging the picture, whose existence the picture implies, is not involved in the action. Rather, in contrast to the crowd depicted in the picture, he remains *contemplator* and *spectator*. Historically considered also, the assumption would contradict the little (relatively) that is known about the collectors and friends for whom Bruegel's works were intended: the cartographer and humanist Ortelius, the rich merchant Nic. Jonghelinck, Cardinal Granvella, or the artists Guilio Clovio, Joris Hoefnagel, etc.

13. Among the many recent authors who emphasize the "contemporary" character of the painting, three may be cited at random. Grossmann, *op. cit.*, p. 199: ". . . Bruegel has here represented the Biblical scene as a contemporary event, a punitive expedition to a Flemish village. . . . The scene is of course based on actual observation." G. Glueck, *Pieter Bruegel le Vieux*, second ed. (Paris: 1936) p. 13: "Quand il trait dans ses tableaux un sujet religieux, il tient à nous donner une image de la vie et cette vie pour lui est celle de son temps." Wolfgang Stechow, *Pieter Bruegel the Elder* (New York: Abrams, 1955) p. 16: "The terrifying Biblical story . . . specifically, has be-

What in the picture makes these various interpretations possible? This possibility derives from a single pictorial element: the fact that precisely that power in the picture which causes the acts of violence or in the name of which they are carried out remains indeterminate and ambiguous. There is no question as to which figure in the "Massacre of the Innocents" embodies the highest power; it is the unarmed dignitary in the center of the picture, the leader or commander of the armored lance-bearers whose group launches the slaughter. Although the role of this figure as the highest authority is clearly designated by his location within the event, although his garments emphatically distinguish him as a non-warrior from the other horsemen, nevertheless the particular nature of his office and of his dignity remains indeterminate. Is it an ecclesiastical or a secular office? A fusion of both?

But since the reality of power, whatever it may be, and its significance can be as little doubted as the reality of the acts of violence and of the helpless victims, the problematic nature and the ambiguity of the central power in the pictorial event point to problems of power-relationships in the historical events of the time. In other words, the objective ambiguity of the pictorial representation appears as the result of the ambiguity or the indeterminateness of the power, or powers, governing historical reality, and thus it becomes a reflection of particular contemporary conditions.[14]

---

come a story of Bruegel's own era. . . . To him, *all* stories from the Bible were events of his own time."

14. The fact that this particular problem-complex of power is dependent on the portrayal of the central dignitary can by chance be proven by an overpainting of Bruegel's "Massacre of the Innocents" executed in the seventeenth century, now located in Hampton Court. (The present author has not seen the picture. A reproduction is found in Grossmann, *op. cit.* Grossmann considers this work to be an original by Bruegel. On this point and on the overpaintings see p. 199 of his book.)

The overpainted version replaces the children's corpses with poultry, pigs, sacks of flour, utensils, etc., and thus transforms the "Massacre of the Innocents" into the representation of a purely military requisition. Here, of course, it is irrelevant to determine why the picture was painted over. Perhaps the murder of the children seemed too gruesome. The only important feature about it is that it also changed the ambiguous figure of the central dignitary. There would have been no reason for this change, however, if the purpose had been only to avoid the horror of the original depiction. The

In what relation does this meaning of the picture, which rests on a detail in the representation and refers to particular historical conditions, stand to the potential content which resulted from the analysis of the pictorial structure and which expressed a general *Zeitgeist*, general historical conditions?

All the essential features of the expressive content—the particular relation between autonomy and independence, between participants and observers, individual and mass, the questionable and unfathomable character of the meaning of the given reality—all these are independent of the pictorial meaning. For they do not derive from the ambiguity of the central power but from the fact that it is only indirectly emphasized as a central power. Its ambiguity, in fact, provides the logical justification for the picture's particular character as "factual report" and as convincing realism.

For the details of every form (an eye, a hand) and every texture (wood, metal) are not depicted with minute precision. It is obviously impossible to read from the picture which specific power conflicts and interests determined the contemporary reality. To give only a few examples, which could easily be multiplied: it is as impossible to deduce from the picture that the (economically) "most typical figure of the sixteenth century [was] the international financier," who used his money impartially to support both the authority of the Pope and that of secular princes at war with each other[15] as it is to deduce that the Antwerp stock exchange was the heart of Europe's finance capitalism[16] until the state bankruptcy of Spain and France in 1557 and of Portugal in 1560 led to a general financial and economic crisis and to the gradual shift of the economic center of gravity to the northern Netherlands.

The power claims of the Spanish monarch in his efforts to

---

central figure now appears, like the mounted men around him, as a fully armored warrior. This dispels any doubt as to the power in the name of which the actions are being carried out. Since the structure of the picture remains the same despite the change in the actions, the expressive content of the picture in the overpainted version remains in principle the same as that of the original although it loses its general power of persuasion and scope by the fact that the depiction is limited to purely military and (in comparison) harmless actions.

15. R. H. Tawney, *Religion and the Rise of Capitalism* (Penguin Books, 1937) p. 65.
16. *Ibid.*, p. 67.

establish a modern centralized administration-system with professional civil servants[17] provoked the resistance of the autonomous provinces, of the cities, and of the high nobility passionately insistent upon the recognition of their inherited privileges, rights, and mores. This resistance also is as little recognizable as the conflict of interests between the high and the lower nobility or the antagonism between the urban oligarchies and the guilds, the revolt of the rural population against the industrial monopolies of the cities, the struggle between economically competing cities, the opposition of the laity against the clergy and the conflicts between Catholics and Protestants, Lutherans and Calvinists. In other words, the intertwined and crisscrossed currents, demands, and conflicts of the period around 1566—local and international, social and political, economic and religious, material and intellectual—the disentangling of which has occupied historians for the last four hundred years, are not distinguished in the picture. Rather, in their totality, they are subsumed as a given fact in the representation and preserved in the ambiguity that surrounds the highest representative of power. In short, the artistic creation condenses and concentrates existing reality, but does not transcend it. Reality is neither glorified nor condemned. Nor is it even explained. Rather, it is described in its incomprehensibility. But perhaps it is for just this reason that the "Massacre of the Innocents" becomes a modern *Lern-und Lehrbild* (a picture instructing and demanding interpretation).[18]

17. "It is strange," the States of Overijssel once said, "that our prince has undertaken to institute new officers and new authorities of which the people have never heard before, a practice never tolerated by the States of the province." "It is strange to conceive," the officers of the Emperor said about the same time in Utrecht, "that His Majesty the Emperor and His servants are not allowed to inflict punishment on one of His subjects, even though an ecclesiastic, without the consent of His other subjects." Cited in B. H. M. Vlekke, *Evolution of the Dutch Nation* (New York: 1945) p. 114.

18. I used this Brechtian concept without knowing that it had also been applied to Bruegel by Ludwig Muenz, *Pieter Bruegel: The Drawings*, translated by Luke Herrmann, Complete Edition (Phaidon Publishers, 1961) p. 29. My translation of the German term follows that given by Herrmann.

# 5.

# Rubens: "The Massacre of the Innocents"

The composition is completely balanced (fig. 9); in the right half of the picture there are glowing colors of bodies and garments in front of a dark palatial building which rises up to the top of the picture; on the left, a gray-black group of figures in front of luminous, softly blended colors of ruins, sky, and landscape. But even before the viewer grasps the picture's compositional construction, he receives the impression of a general flowing motion, like a rhythmic falling and rising, and the impact of the painting as an immediately convincing, sensuous, living reality of passionate happenings becomes evident before the eye recognizes the details of the representation.

People completely dominate the scene. Three clearly distinguished main groups fill the whole width. In its center, in relative isolation, stands a richly dressed female figure in a dramatic pose of helpless distress. Is she the "heroine" or even a main protagonist of the action? In any case, she is the pivotal point of the whole composition since her figure connects and separates at once the two halves of the picture and the various groups represented coloristically, expressively, and with regard to the dominant directions of movement.

The train of this figure's black garment merges with the shabby skirts of the two women to her left, who in wild fury use their nails to fight the executioners who tear their children away from them, killing them. Simultaneously, however, the bright red and orange of her ermine-trimmed dress and the yellow of its shimmering silk lining connect her also with the lamenting women on the steps to her right. Save for the black (which Rubens uses as a color), all the colors which compose her magnificent clothing are repeated—or echoed and varied with complementary colors—in the equally sumptuous garments of those

9. *The Massacre of the Innocents* by Rubens [Bayerische Staatsgemäldesammlungen, München]

women.[1] And a similar richness of color, which produces a truly festive effect, also characterizes the large principal group on the right. Its optic center is a radiant yellow,[2] the same yellow which suffuses the figure in the center of the picture.

Although the figure in the center is closely linked coloristically to the right main group and to the women immediately adjoining her on both sides, she just as distinctly divides them from each other. The powerful downward thrust which starts in two diagonals[3] at the left edge of the picture and, in its lower part, traverses the two enraged women, terminates in the black train of her dress. At the same time her slightly turned posture forms the point of departure for the picture's great upward thrust toward the right. A rising diagonal, this movement passes first through the lamenting women and the executioners on the steps and then continues up to the corner pillar near the right edge (middle ground). A notice that probably decrees the massacre is posted on the pillar against which the murderers fling their victims. It is only at this point that a great counterthrust begins: cataract-like its movement falls, from the corpses of the children hanging over the balustrade, passing through the groups of women and soldiers interlocked in furious struggle, down to the woman lying on her back in the immediate foreground to the right. The horizontal of her body leads the eye back to the figure in the center[4] from which the diagonal upward

1. The pigeon-blue dress of the woman fervently pressing a dead child to her bosom has yellow sleeves and red-orange modeling and a pure red appears as coloristic accent on the child's sheet; the woman extending her arms in an imploring gesture wears a green dress with yellow highlights, etc.

2. The silk skirt of the standing seminude figure seen from the back.

3. A steep diagonal begins in the upper left-hand corner of the picture. It cuts through the corner of the ruin, the upper part of the shaft of the column, and the head and shoulder of the woman scratching the executioner's face, and touches the line of the back of the other woman who is fighting the executioner with her. The second diagonal, which is less steep, begins in the hand of the executioner at the picture's left edge, who is pointing his sword, and traverses the right shoulder and left arm of the executioner seen frontally. It then cuts through the chin, torso, and elbow of the sitting woman fighting him and leads to the same terminal point as the first diagonal.

4. The two opposing thrusts in the right half of the picture and the groups forming them thus produce an oval, the apices of which lie approximately in the children's corpses at the pillar and between the central

thrust started. Thus, the central figure becomes the terminal and turning point alike of the dramatic downward thrust. In other words, in her figure merge all the contrasting directions underlying the abstract formal organization of the work into three great main groups, each of which constitutes a geometrical pattern.[5]

While linking the groups and the women next to her coloristically, she thereby formally divides them. Nor is that all. The attitude of the lady of quality and her companions in sorrow on the steps, still "beautiful" even in deep pain, are worlds apart from the savagery of the poor women of the people who actively resist the executioners, sinking their teeth into their flesh, tearing at their hair, scratching their faces and bodies in horrible raging fury.[6] The stark contrast in dress worn by the women explains their different behavior as a difference in social rank and the whole picture is permeated by the details in keeping with this distinction.[7]

Thus, it is only with the similarly sumptuously garbed ladies of quality on the steps that the central figure forms a fully integrated group, both in terms of expression and movement. As in her gesture of helplessness, these women also express their suffering in incontrollable distraught lamentations and desperate imploring gesticulations, but not by direct bodily resistance.[8]

In this way the battling women of the left and right groups

---

figure and the feet of the woman fighting on her back. The compositional importance of this oval, however, is lesser than that of the geometric figures on which the three main groups are based. For color accents emphasize individual figures to such a degree (above all the standing woman in yellow seen from the back) that their lines of movement greatly tone down, if not destroy, the effect of the oval. In a black-and-white reproduction the oval is easily discernible.

5. On the left an almost mathematically perfect right-angle triangle; in the middle a quadrangle; on the right an isosceles triangle or a pyramid. Many individual figures, or figures forming subgroups, also correspond to mathematical shapes, which will not be described here in detail.

6. Near the right edge of the picture in the middle ground; right foreground; left foreground.

7. For example, the disheveled hair or the hairdos interlaced with jewels; sinewy arms or pliant full limbs, etc.

8. Likewise the gesture of the aforementioned standing figure seen from the back, defined as a member of the upper social ranks by her yellow silk skirt and careful hairdo, is in keeping with the group in the center.

become an expressive unit as contrasted to that of the central group just as they formally had been contrasted to it by the downward diagonals which delimit the groups. And yet there is no doubt that one and the same extreme emotion, common to all the women, governs their behavior, no matter how much its manifestations may vary. No single woman is a "heroine." Rather, the instantaneously engendered effect of *all* the women as the collective bearer of expression outweighs the multiplicity of individual forms in which the expressive content is concretized and differentiated. In other words, it is evident that the distinction between the women as representatives of upper and lower social ranks serves only to endow their different behavior with a rational motivation. The intensity of expression they embody is altogether prior to this distinction and unaffected by it.

The degree to which the despairing women dominate the picture is shown particularly by the fact that, in comparison, even the executioners seem like stage extras although it is they and their deeds that are crucial for the meaning of the work. Indeed it would hardly be an exaggeration to say that it is only gradually that the viewer "discovers" most of the henchmen among the women even though the latter do not outnumber them.[9] The women give the impression of a much larger "crowd" because only the two executioners in the left foreground are shown full length. All the other murderers are either largely overlapped by female figures[10] or smaller in scale.[11]

With the exception of the group on the left, furthermore, the executioners nowhere determine the point of departure of dominant directional movements; rather, in each case they are merely continuations of directions which begin in the female figures.[12] The short

9. Apart from the figure of the executioner almost completely hidden by the corner pillar and the figure of the maid (only her head and arm are visible) supporting the woman with the dead child on the steps there are eleven executioners and soldiers and eleven women.

10. The soldiers on the steps and the executioners entangled with the fighting mothers on the right.

11. For example, the half-naked figure, laden with children's corpses, hurrying to throw his burden on the pile of corpses in the palace.

12. In the large descending diagonal of the right group, for example, coloristically it is the woman directly under the corner pillar and the woman on her back in the foreground, both in bright blue, who form the starting and terminal points of the main thrust and not the executioners who are struggling with them.

leftward-falling diagonal created by the armored soldiers on the steps also serves to underline, rather than counteract, the rising movement in the opposite direction created by the ladies of quality who plead for mercy in front of them.[13] It thus strengthens the general impression of wavelike motion evoked by the picture, but it does not determinate the direction of movement.

Coloristically, too, the henchmen and the soldiers are never the exponents of the colors most important in the composition: none of the men is comparable in degree and intensity of color treatment to the dominant effect of the blacks, yellows, reds, etc. of the women. In a certain sense here too the left group represents an exception: it is indispensable for the light-dark balance of the composition and the two executioners are as "rich" in color as the mothers battling them.[14] Optically, however, they remain closely linked with all the other murderers strewn throughout the picture because they, like their fellows, are dark in comparison to the other figures in the picture. Nevertheless, the strongest and purest color in that group is neither in the figures of the executioners nor in those of the mothers: it is found in the red pool of blood on the ground, being lapped up by a black dog.

Thus the executioners are without doubt compositionally subordinate to the women. Indeed precisely for this reason they confront them as an expressive unit deriving directly from the structure of the painting and *not* from their deeds. But this statement neither defines nor exhausts the particular nature of the contrast any more than would the further statement that the deeds of the executioners set off the women's behavior. The work was intended to be seen at close range. And indeed only careful observation discloses, in the details of the characterizations of the murderers and the women, the reason for the contrast in expression between them. In themselves, the faces and bodies of the executioners are by no means "uglier" or more repulsive than those of the women who are attacking them in brutal desperation. But the mothers alone appear as fully individualized persons, physically and

13. Its thrust is all the less because in the continuation of the lowered partisans it immediately encounters the much stronger counterthrust of the left main group and comes to a standstill at the head of the fighting woman.

14. Yellowish, orange, and greenish tones predominate in the modelings of their bodies. The flesh colors of the women show more pink.

spiritually. Each face has its own expression of torment, pain, or mad-
ness, distinguishing it from all the others, and the individually differentiated features, whether in helpless distress or distorted by rage, go
hand in hand with differentiations in physical appearance and gestures.

In contrast to this profusion of detailed psychological and
physiognomical characterization of the women, the depiction of the
murderers emphasizes only their physical strength. To be sure, their
faces are not altogether blank. The brutality and coarseness of their expression is wholly in keeping with the grim energy of their violent
deeds. But just as the features of all the executioners and soldiers are
essentially *the same*, distinguished from one another only by slight and
purely external characteristics (bearded or beardless, for example), so
do they all wear the same expression.[15] In other words, it is not the
coarseness of their expression but the lack of any personal expression
that marks the inhumanity of the murderers, underlining and explain-
ing their deep contrast to the mothers, who display human feelings
even in their inhuman acts.

The avoidance of individual differentiation in the faces of the
executioners is all the more striking since their athletic figures, where
they are fully visible in prominent places, show the same detailed, penetrating description of textures as those of the women. Their hard mus-
culature, modeled with great precision, contrasts with the soft bodies
of the children and the flesh of the bared breasts; the bloody scratches
on the face of the executioner in the left group are shown as clearly as
the bleeding hand of the woman in the right foreground who grabs the
blade of a dagger.

But details of this kind, which underline the bloodthirsty
gruesomeness of the theme, are rare in the over-all picture. It is a characteristic feature of the work (and important for its expressive content)
that the various gruesome aspects of the representation, despite all the
realistic details, are not decisive optically either in the picture as a
whole or at close range. This is due not only to the sensuous splendor
of the color, predominant in determining the immediate effect of the
whole and preceding any differentiation, but above all to the way color

15. Compare, for example, the three female figures in the left
group, physically and psychologically so different from one another, with
the two executioners in the same group. Or the soldiers on the steps with
the women in front of them.

is used as a descriptive means. For the particular textures of the objects shown are not all presented with the same intensity and clarity. Thus the glowing flesh of the bodies overflowing with vitality is emphasized, as is the gleam of silk, the muted shimmer of metal, the glistening of a tear or of a jewel, and the contrast between smooth marble and rough stone. The murdered children, however, scarcely show a wound and seem to be asleep rather than dead.

In other words, although the horrendous aspects are not eliminated from the representation, they are systematically weakened and their effects softened by this differential treatment of textures. The group on the left offers a particularly clear example of this. It is the only instance in the picture where the viewer sees the murder of a child at the moment of its perpetration.[16] And several children's corpses lie on the blood-soaked ground. In the context of the scene, indeed, the glaringly bright red at the feet of the executioners can *signify* only blood; it is important to note, however, that this red is *not* realistically rendered as blood but rather as pure pigmentation.[17] On the other hand, while color on the infant corpses is used in a realistically descriptive way, it primarily depicts the softness of their bodies and the delicacy of their blond and brown locks. In short, the realism emphasizes the physical loveliness of the victims, not the violence of their death.

Not only are the most brutal scenes and actions always shown in a way that prevents their optical predominance, but the instigators of the horrible deeds also remain "in the dark" in the truest sense of the word: two seated half-length figures, almost hidden, can be seen inside the palace at the extreme right of the picture, directly behind the pillar where the executioners are making a bloody heap of the corpses (this heap, too, is small and not emphasized). Thus the instigators are perceptible, but in comparison to the other figures in the picture they appear indistinct and almost shadowlike.

In terms of the picture's meaning there is no emphasis placed

16. Hans G. Evers in *Peter Paul Rubens*, Bruckmann, 1942, p. 415, expresses astonishment that Rubens could create the "Massacre of the Innocents" while his own children were playing at his feet and he illustrates the brutality of the depiction with the above-mentioned detail. But he fails to point out that this scene is the only one of its kind in the picture that can be seen clearly.

17. Broad horizontal brush strokes whose parallelism and more or less regular spacing is not at all "descriptive."

either on those figures who are in fact—but not optically!—the point of departure of the representation nor on those who complete the work in the religious sense: the celestial beings in the upper left half of the painting who, with flowers and wreaths, are intended to signify the salvation and reward of the innocents. As in the depiction of the women and the executioners, here too the elements of expression and meaning do not coincide with the structure of the painting.[18]

This fact explains why it is impossible to give a narrative description of the "Massacre of the Innocents" based on the sequence of the picture's visual impact. Such a description is all the less possible because, its perfect artistic unity notwithstanding, the painting does not present a unified action. Rather, the different figures and groups of figures underline a multiplicity of individual actions, each of which is so motivated by the artist that they are rationally—but again, not optically—independent of one another and comprehensible without regard to the whole.[19] But despite the logical motivations so carefully provided for every individual action and gesture[20]—or precisely because of these motivations—the actions seem to be the effect not of an event specifically determined by one specific cause but rather the result and expression of a general arousal of the senses and feelings raised to the highest pitch. In short, the "Massacre of the Innocents" does not deal with the description of a unified event but with "making visible" a single psychic state: human passion.

18. And yet what Burckhardt says *in general* about the equivalence of the visual and the moral element in the work of Rubens is correct. In this case, not only are Herod and his companion in the dark and the angels in the light, but the angels are also completely "free," unconfined by any other forms, whereas Herod (or his representative) seems to be imprisoned by the pillars, balustrade, architrave, etc.

19. Each of the three main groups forms such an autonomous unit of action, and within each group other logically independent figures can be distinguished: for example, the woman in black on the ground throwing herself over her dead child (left group), the imploring figure in the center of the picture, and the various groups of which the main group on the right is composed.

20. The attitude of the despairing mother in black, for example, is explained by her dead child; but she herself, in turn, motivates, although almost too obviously, the postures of the two fighting executioners, who, without her would be suspended in the air. Coloristically, however, the same woman cannot be separated from the group as a whole. Or the inconspicuous figures of the two men holding stones who, left of center, effect the transi-

Passion as such is the basic effect of Rubens' humanity, its elemental state of being, as it were, a state which, in principle, is unconditioned and, though prior to all particular situations, suffuses them all. Neither the specific (religious) meaning nor the individual actions explain the painting's particular pathos. This pathos stems from the intensity of the optical-sensuous effect produced by the work. Passion, as a general, rationally irreducible affect appears in the picture not as the sum of various passionate manifestations (raging fury, helpless despair, etc.); rather, these manifestations, conversely, appear as so many various "modes" of passion as such, each of which is factually, psychologically, formally—in short, rationally explained and motivated by the artist.

In other words, just as the over-all composition and total effect of the picture, essentially based on color, are "calmed down" (Burckhardt) and articulated through the abstract-geometrical patterns, so do its optical-sensuous elements, whose impact is prior to all differentiations, stress the irrational, emotional character of human nature. In the actions, gestures, postures of all the figures, however, human nature is subjected to the insight of reason through the aforementioned rational motivations.

Obviously, the picture's structure is thus based on the combination of two entirely different artistic means which are recognizable as such throughout the work. But does it necessarily follow therefrom that both are of equal importance for the expressive content of the "Massacre of the Innocents" or that each of them has a fundamentally different expressive character? Is their interrelationship in the picture altogether clearly defined? Were this fundamental distinction between the sensuous (irrational) and the abstract-formal (rational) elements of the picture not made, would the painting lose its objective expressive character? Does the meaning of the picture provide a hint to their relationship? No viewer, without possessing extra-artistic historical knowl-

---

tion to the background of the picture. Their function, in fact, is purely compositional, namely, to prevent a funnel-effect in the background. But because the artist depicts them as making threatening gestures and equips them with stones as weapons, they are characterized as fathers or brothers fighting a losing battle against an overpowerful enemy. Thus their action is as objectively clear as it is optically understated.

edge, could directly infer from the structure of the picture that beyond its religious meaning the painting was calculated to satisfy the demands of the educated (contemporary) "amateur." The demonstration of this posits the ability to discern the classical details and "quotations" of the work, culled from the ideas current in the world of antiquarian-humanistic culture. To cite but a few examples: the different "antique" architectures of the ruins, the baptistery, and the palace; the Laocoon-like figure of the executioner in the left group; the woman on her back fighting in the foreground, probably taken from Titian's "Europa" (Boston) or a direct imitation of a Roman-Hellenistic sculpture ("Fighting Gaul," Palace of the Doges, Venice);[21] the figure in the center of the painting which more or less recalls the famous Niobe (in the Uffizi, Florence).

Hence it is no accident that precisely these three figures which so clearly point to the knowledge of the cultured beholders are strongly emphasized in the compositional structure. The appeal to the contemporary connoisseur's intellectual and aesthetic capacity for enjoyment corresponds furthermore to the separation of the elements which are the vehicles of the religious meaning from those conveying the artistic expression, a separation already disclosed in the structural analysis of the work.

But this aesthetic-humanistic meaning, above all, confirms and underlines the importance of the distinction made between the rational and the irrational elements in the picture. For only viewers who do not primarily "identify" with the excited actors in the events depicted but who, rather, stand *above* the passions shown are capable of perceiving and judging the utilization of such "cultural elements."

Likewise, only those viewers able in principle to make a distinction between affects, emotions and considered action, self-control, and reason can weigh, in terms of form and content, the truth in the representation of passions and enjoy it as in the unfolding of a classical drama.

Nevertheless, the painting also offers the possibility for a

21. It is for the specialists to decide whether still other figures are direct or indirect imitations of ancient statues, cameos, sarcophagi, etc., which no doubt were known to the art lover of the time. The soldier fighting with the woman on her back in the foreground, for example, bears a resemblance to the upper "wrestler" in the "Wrestler" group in the Uffizi and

contemporary beholder to grasp the picture exclusively in terms of its most immediate effect which is based essentially on feeling. But in that case the feeling relates only to the sensuous, affective, material elements of the representation and to its religious meaning which inevitably leads the beholder to identify with and re-live the passions portrayed and to be overcome by them, so that he himself is dominated by affects. Thereby, the distinction between rational and irrational artistic means not only would no longer obtain but the more the beholder emotionally identifies with the scenes and the protagonists, the more unimportant the "cultural elements," so expressly stressed by the artist, are bound to become—if he perceives and notices them at all.

Thus, actually there are two different ways of conceiving and experiencing the work, two ways which are not only different in degree but in kind and which do not intersect. But although it *seems* as if the two ways depend on the knowledge of the beholder, this is not simply a matter of the truism that every work of art "is multi-leveled" and every beholder "sees only what he knows." For the difference of the two conceptions can be made only because the elements of both possibilities of expression are actually inherent in the structure of the work independently from one another.

Thus, it is not the humanistic-aesthetic or the affective-religious *meaning* of the "Massacre of the Innocents" that determines the possible effects sketched above. Conversely, rather, both are a consequence of that problem which, for the moment, perhaps best circumscribes the expressive content of the painting: the problem concerning the relationship between "nature" and "reason," "passion" and "ratio," and which also includes that of the role and the characteristics of reason.

This may sound abstract. It has been noted, however, that the geometrical patterns underlying the three main groups of the painting do in fact articulate the composition as a whole and that the rationally intelligible motivations explain the various actions depicted. To this extent, therefore, ratio, in contradistinction to the sensuous elements, undoubtedly represents a principle of order. But is this reason

---

the woman and the soldier recall Daniele de Volterra's "Massacre of the Innocents" in SS. Trinità dei Monti in Rome.

divine or human? In terms of its visible aspects alone the picture does not answer the question, inasmuch as the mere intensity of material being and passion as such cannot necessarily be interpreted as cause, manifestation, or aim of supernatural forces. But if the causal connection of the phenomena depicted is inaccessible to (human) reason, the latter turns into an instrument of a purely formal order which does not permeate the emotional, sensuous, irrational being but merely "regulates" or "controls" it from without, as it were.

Manifestly these remarks do not allow any conclusions to be drawn regarding the individual piety of the beholders (let alone of the artist!). They do point, however, to a general conception of religious matters or to a religious attitude which apprehends the divine and its operation as being fundamentally removed from the faculty of human reason, that is, rational insight. "Divine reason" is altogether incommensurable with human understanding. No leap of thought, however daring, can open the way to the divine and the doctrines of the Church, but only faith, the subjective uplift of feeling that unconditionally submits to what is beyond the grasp of rationality.

This basic delimitation of human reason in relation to the divine becomes evident not only through the separation between the aforementioned vehicles of expression and meaning. It is no less clearly indicated by the fact—itself a result of this very separation—that the "purely artistic" character of the work is objectively (optically) accentuated more strongly than the religious story.[22] For precisely to the extent that reason is declared incompetent to understand or prove the truths proclaimed by the Church, it becomes an independent faculty of knowledge which follows its own laws. In this way, however, reason can determine the goal of knowledge subjectively, whereby the claim to truth no longer necessarily finds its justification in the cognized object but in the process of cognition.

---

22. In another context, with no particular reference to the "Massacre of the Innocents," G. Jedlicka says, "Rubens no longer creates from a tension in relation to the subject; he is already creating from a tension exclusively in relation to form." In *Pieter Bruegel* (Erlenbach, 1938) p. 450 R. Oldenbourg had previously made similar remarks in *Peter Paul Rubens* (Munich-Berlin: 1922). For example, p. 130: "This sovereign distance from the subject . . ."

This is not tantamount to asserting that the transformation of reason into an autonomous faculty, perceptible as a possibility in the "Massacre of the Innocents," points *directly* and *unambiguously* to definite concepts such as "raison d'état," Jesuit religiosity, or political absolutism. Nevertheless, it can hardly be denied that the problem of the secularization of reason is only a particular aspect of the concrete political, religious, and economic power-conflicts which pervasively marked the entire seventeenth century, in fact from about the second half of the sixteenth century to the absolutist State perfected under Louis XIV. Thus it is understandable that the expressive content of the "Massacre of the Innocents" corresponds, or could correspond, on the one hand, to a religious world view which employs subjective rationality as a psychological instrument to attain an irrational goal *(propaganda fides)* and, on the other, to world views which—in intrinsically very different ways—rationalize and thereby theoretically justify secular claims to power or to (fundamentally irrational) "absolute" power as such (Botero's "raison d'état," Bacon's "knowledge is power," Hobbes' "philosophy of power," the monopolistic economic theories of mercantilism, etc.).

No conclusions by analogy are needed, however, to recognize that the painting in its depiction of human beings as well as in its emphasis on the sensuous-material being as such posits a conception of man that acknowledges his corporeality (and the reality of the material world) as fully as his mental, emotional, or spiritual nature.[23] But that does not say much, because such a generalization could be made about many different societies (before and after Rubens' time) that have produced works of art wholly different in appearance and different in expressive content. How does this basic equal valuation of physical and psychic reality appear in the "Massacre of the Innocents"?

No other factor but the material, sensuous, and affective being is emphasized in the painting. In the representation of human passion the sensuous world and the affects, raised to peak intensity, are fused into an indissoluble unity. Rubens' people exist uniquely, as passionate and thus "unproblematic" beings in a purely sensuous

---

23. It is probably superfluous to remark that, regardless of the individual artistic talent, such a conception cannot be engendered by a single artist of genius but only by a generally shared mental attitude.

world. A conflict between their corporeality, their feelings, and their actions (as in the work of the mature and late Michelangelo, or in El Greco's dematerialized figures) is inconceivable.

To be sure the "Massacre of the Innocents" presupposes a society or a public that is keenly interested in the nature or the psychology of passion and whose interest, furthermore, is oriented more toward the individual personality than toward the anonymous masses or an abstract societally normative ideal type. Thus, as previously shown, all the figures are depicted as distinct individualities—more precisely, as bearers of different aspects of passion—and each is designed to be seen in its physiognomic or bodily uniqueness. It is for this reason, though the work represents a mass scene, that each figure, as a vehicle of expression, preserves its individual importance and autonomy. And yet in the picture as a whole the individual figures are not of equal value *formally*, since those in the larger groups (and their subgroups) are always dominated by *one* main figure. Thus the sensuous-irrational elements of the picture, which underlie the work's fundamental unity and determine its material splendor and its pathos, emphasize the kindred nature and thereby the essential equality of the people represented. On the other hand, the various individuals are treated according to the principle of formal subordination or accentuated in comparison to the others by the abstract-geometrical structural elements of the composition. The word "formal" is crucial here. For the instinctual-organic force equally embodied in all the figures is as unaffected by this formal inequality as the condition of pathos, common to all the women, is by the emphasis on distinction in social rank.

The contrast between the structural sensuous-irrational and the rational-formal elements which characterizes the expressive content loses none of its importance, although unreflected, sensuous "nature" powerfully dominates the picture. The very fact that passion is depicted as an (irrational) natural phenomenon whereas the representation is intended to appeal to the rational capacities of the beholder implies the confrontation between the autonomous pictorial world, created by the artist, and the real world of the viewer. The contrast between "nature" and "reason," "passion" and "ratio" is thus repeated as the contrast between art and reality.

But what kind of reality is at issue here? Does the expressive content refer to a "rational" historical world? By no means. Its immediate impact is that of a deep-rooted dualistic world view, which sunders "nature" and "reason," establishing them as fundamentally different spheres of reality. Not even the mediation of subjective reason overcomes this dualism. For the function of human reason perforce is restricted to the recognition of its own opposition to "pure nature" as shown in the autonomous reality of the painting. If, however, the concrete beholder becomes conscious of the irrational character of this "nature," he is compelled to concede its efficacy in the historical world as an independent overriding force. In other words, as a human faculty, reason's superiority to "nature" is, in principle, of a conditioned character only.

But why, despite this dualism, is there no suggestion of a threatening or painful conflict? The answer lies precisely in the aforementioned dialectical reciprocal relation between the picture's artistic reality and historical reality. For if the pictorial world in its "natural" unity stands, on the one hand, altogether outside the dualism depicted and is emphatically independent of the viewer's world, on the other, however, it refers not only to a "rational" viewer but also represents elements of objective reality. The "rational" viewer, however, can not only aesthetically enjoy this depicted objective reality; he can dominate it through *reason*. And precisely this imaginary mastery of the real world, made possible by the structure of the picture and consummated in the picture, explains why the dualism of nature and reason, art and reality, does not acquire the character of conflict: in the "Massacre of the Innocents" the relation between the concrete viewer and the dualistic world around him is idealized. The sensuous charm and material splendor of the picture, far from spiritualizing the real world or removing the viewer from it, confirm his imaginary reconciliation and seeming domination of objective reality. In other words, the "Massacre of the Innocents" does not oppose to the real world an ideal world, in which the opposition of nature and reason would be reconciled and surmounted through mutual interpenetration. Rather, the dualistic expressive content points to a historical situation in which mastery of the world and of man through subjective reason is not generally realized but appears realizable to the rational individual. But since the world is presented in such sensuous magnificence while its gruesome aspects are muted, the "Massacre of the Innocents" likewise indicates that the concrete individual, instead of wanting, even theoretically, to bring about a world in which reason and reality interpenetrate, is far more interested in the concrete mastery of the existing "irrational" reality with the help of his subjective reason, in order to enjoy it.

# 6.

## Results of the Analyses

### EXPRESSIVE CONTENT AND OBJECTIVE VALUE JUDGMENTS

The preceding analyses have shown that the extra-artistic, time-bound character of works of art appears independently of iconographic meaning in the socially conditioned expressive content. The structure and, in varying degrees, content of different societies or social strata prove to be constitutive elements of visual form-relationships; that is, they inhere in the expressive content.

Can this be of help in answering the questions: why were the described (or other) works evaluated differently at different times in history? And why will this necessarily continue to be the case? Presumably the different judgments result, directly or indirectly, from the relation between the inherent expressive content and the world view of the beholder, which is also historically conditioned. Thus admiration for or rejection of the works would depend on whether and to what extent the expressive content actually or seemingly corresponds to the mental attitudes of the viewers which are evaluated, positively or negatively, in every historical situation. It must be borne in mind, however, that a positive judgment does not presuppose exact analogies between social conditions and world views of the period in which the work was created and those obtaining in the period in which the viewer is living. The assumption here, rather, is that the expressive content preserves its time-conditioned efficacy in changed historical conditions and essentially determines the judgment of the work even though the viewer may not be conscious of this fact.

The history of the judgments about Giotto (and the Italian "primitives" in general) confirms this assumption. In fact, the dependence of the changing value judgments on the expressive content is so clearly discernible in the example of Giotto that it is possible to dispense here with an empirical demonstration of the same fact with respect to Bruegel and Rubens.[1]

To be sure, all judgments about Giotto which do not make a positive or negative evaluation of his particular artistic style have no bearing on the methodological problem under discussion here—for example, those stressing his chronological importance as the ancestor of a new epoch in art history or considering his works as an instructive example of the history of costumes and architecture. It is well known that for the most part these criteria still prevailed throughout the seventeenth century just as for Vasari Giotto's artistic greatness was not absolute but entirely relative in comparison to the achievements of later masters. In the eighteenth century, however, this was supplanted by a fundamental reevaluation of Giotto and his immediate successors[2] in which the connection between the rationalistic expressive content of his art and the new spirit of the Enlightenment is unmistakable. This connection is all the more unmistakable in that Giotto's artistic value is emphasized (and in part expressly contrasted with the "artificial," "exaggerated," and "untrue," that is, "unnatural" quality of "modern" and late Baroque art)[3] even when the critic's personal taste (Muratori's, for example) still fundamentally resists this "early" art.[4] In other words, in the eighteenth century, "simplicity" and "truth" (in the sense of "truth to nature") are increasingly recognized *and* praised as the essential expressive content of Giotto's art; for the rational connotation of his work evoked by these concepts represents

---

1. It is beyond the scope of the present study to show this with respect to these two artists. For it is certainly possible to regard the pervasive rationalism and the ideal character, based on that rationalism, of Giotto's "Massacre of the Innocents" as *the* expressive content of his art as such which achieved even greater depth, for example, in his later frescoes in Santa Croce. A similar generalization, however, is excluded both in Bruegel and Rubens since the expressive content of the works described here differs from that of the earlier works of these artists not only in degree but fundamentally. Thus one would have to make a careful study to determine whether the change in their evaluation, in each case, concerns the same or completely different expressive aspects of their art.

2. See G. Previtali, *La Fortuna dei Primitivi. Dal Vasari ai Neoclassici* (Turin: Einaudi, 1964) p. 58.

3. *Ibid.*, p. 77, especially notes 1 and 2, and p. 95 ff.

4. *Ibid.*, pp. 74–5.

a positive value within the historical situation of the Enlightenment.[5]
But when this rationality loses its positive connotation, the evaluation
of the work in which it appears is likewise negatively evaluated. Thus
the "enlightened" Italian scholar Lanzi writes in 1789 that through
Giotto painting for the first time became capable of *appropriately*
handling *all* themes.[6] In 1827, however, the Romanticist Rumohr as-
serts that the decline of religious art begins with Giotto: the "coldness
of his intellect, his clarity of mind" resist "that enthusiastic and total
self-surrender . . . without which seemingly nothing lofty and digni-
fied can be wrought."[7]

The examples given suffice to answer the question why the
evaluation of the same work of art *must necessarily* change in the
course of history: the necessity results from the interplay between the
historically conditioned nature of the expressive content and the historically conditioned nature of the judgments. But this explanation
also leads to a more precise determination of the concept of "timelessness" or the "timeless value" of great works of art. Obviously the
quality—the "timeless value"—of a work is demonstrated not by the
content of the frequently contradictory judgments but by the fact that
it continues to evoke these changing value judgments or virtually con-
tains them. In other words, the artistic quality can be objectively
demonstrated in the expressive content or as the potential expressive
content. The proof of this assertion inevitably rests on a kind of vicious
circle since it is impossible to foresee the effect of the expressive con-

---

5. The fundamental significance of this new evaluation of Giotto's
art on the basis of its rationalistic expressive content, as evidenced in the
writings of an ever growing number of "enlightened" scholars and connoisseurs, is not diminished in the slightest by the fact that this new evaluation
can by no means be taken as a sign of a *general* and all-embracing change
in taste. A few passages from letters written in 1739-40 by President Charles
de Brosses, whose level of culture is incontestable, suffice to prove the contrary: ". . . Cimabue's "Madonna" . . . which is probably the earliest picture
of the Florentine school, seems to me not unworthy of a game-room painter.
The picture . . . has no drawing, no plastic effect, no coloring. It consists only
of a badly drawn line smeared with various colors; the paintings of Giotto,
Cimabue's follower, are much better, although very bad." "This great master [Giotto] so highly praised in all our history books, today would not be
allowed to decorate a game-room." Quotations from Previtali, *op. cit.*, p. 205.
6. Previtali, *ibid.*, p. 145; E. Cecchi, *Giotto* (Milan: 1937) p. 133.
7. Quoted in W. Hausenstein, *Giotto* (Berlin: 1923) p. 158.

tent on societies not yet in existence. (For this reason any speculation on the "art of the future" is absurd!)

Yet the same fact explains why the "judgments of posterity" (not *the* judgment of posterity) are by no means "more correct" than the evaluations which the expressive content of the work elicited from its contemporary viewers. Of course, the question as to the objective validity of judgments can be discussed only once it is known whether the different judgments actually refer to the artistic quality present as expressive content in the visual form-relationships of the work or whether they are determined by wholly other criteria which have nothing to do with artistic quality (historical or iconographic meaning, rarity, novelty, etc.). Elsewhere it has been shown that these criteria are for their part variable and depend to a great extent on the socially conditioned functions that painting or other types of art fulfill, or are supposed to fulfill, at a given time. The insight that such criteria bear no relation to the artistic quality of the work (although they influence its evaluation) makes comprehensible why paintings (both old and new) which are the most "short-lived" are precisely those whose contemporary fame rests primarily, if not exclusively, on the elements of meaning which are never immanent to the work of art. (This is shown very clearly by the results of iconographic and iconological research.)

Thus the distinction between meaning and expression leads to the seeming paradox that the potential impact of a picture, that is, its "timelessness," becomes all the more improbable to the extent that the work lives exclusively from the elements of meaning represented in it; whereas, conversely, the time-bound character of a work, as it appears in the immanence of the expressive content, guarantees and proves its "timeless" quality.[8]

This contradiction is resolved by the fact that in the expressive content deeper and more comprehensive aspects of human existence are revealed because the social reality—different in each case—which conditions the historical existence of every individual is artistically grasped and developed as an independent totality. Whereas ele-

8. For this reason the meaning of a work does not change its essential expressive content even though at the time of its creation it was "meant" not "solemnly" but "jocularly." Cf. E. Wind, *Bellini's Feast of The Gods* (Harvard University Press, 1948).

ments of meaning by their very nature always refer exclusively to particular and frequently unique historical facts and circumstances without which their appearance in the picture is incomprehensible, the expressive content as the picture's visual appearance explains the historical reality which constitutes its presupposition and its basis. But at the same time the expressive content outstrips this particular reality. The potential impact particular to it becomes actuality in the reciprocal relation between the painting and the beholder. The more the original historical reality has been absorbed into the work, the higher its quality.

The greater or lesser *richness* and *scope* of philosophical (social) contents—*not* their specific character—are taken as the criterion of artistic quality. As a result the comparison of the expressive content of individual works of art, whose uniqueness is thus not only respected but emphasized, offers the possibility of an objective evaluation of differences of artistic quality: for the depth and profusion of conceptions of world and man which the individual works contain can be "gleaned" from the visible given forms and form-relations.[9]

Such comparison of unique, that is, intrinsically "incomparable," objects is methodologically justified and not self-contradictory because the expressive content itself is the *tertium comparationis*. Rather, it is only in this way that art history and art criticism can meaningfully pose and resolve the crucial question of the comparability of works of art, a question which the "pure" history of styles answers unsatisfactorily by only referring to similarities or differences in formal characteristics.

---

9. The fact that the necessary presupposition, namely, the "ability to see," is unfortunately by no means generally fulfilled cannot be raised as an objection to the method proposed here even though there is a close connection between this regrettable fact and the unsatisfactory findings of present-day research in art history and art criticism with respect to an understanding of art, stressed at the beginning of this study. Cf. Kurt Badt's reflections, which are very similar, in *"Modell und Maler,"* von Jan Vermeer, DuMont Dokumente, Texte und Perspektiven, (Cologne: 1961) note p. 82: "Leonardo's 'sapere videre' is also our chief problem. It seems to me that a main reason for the fact that art history—for all its merits—has contributed relatively little to the understanding of what is artistically significant in a work of art, lies in the lack of objective observation of what is *artistically* represented (which is something different from the subject matter *actually* represented)."

## EXPRESSIVE CONTENT AND HISTORY OF STYLES

This criterion of the relative complexity or poverty of expressive content, as determined through comparison, is practically applicable to all epochs of art history, present or past. For such comparison can demonstrate the higher artistic quality of Giotto compared to the "Giottesques," for example, or of Rubens to Jacob Jordaens. At the same time it can preserve the "value-free" character of purely descriptive stylistic concepts (such as Woelfflin's "linear" and "painterly") as well as purely classificatory concepts such as early Renaissance or analytical cubism.

The possibility and validity of such a comparison, however, is by no means restricted to works of art which display the same formal charactertistics. For the historically conditioned character of the potential expressive content is manifested precisely in the particular way with which the unity of "form" and "expression" is realized in every work of art. And it is this unity which constitutes the very definition of the potential content. Therefore the demonstration of the inherently social (ideological) character of the expressive content, attempted in the preceding analyses, does more than merely change and complement the problems posed by the history of styles. Above all it refutes that assumption which, as previously indicated, is tacitly or explicitly posited by the pure history of styles, namely, that works of art exhibiting the same method in the combination of the same formal elements—whether they belong to the same time or to entirely different periods (periodicity)— for this very reason always correspond to or spring from mental attitudes, a "life-stance," or world views which are fundamentally alike.[10]

10. Certainly not only the enormous accumulation of art-historical material but this assumption itself has furthered the extremely important insight into the contemporaneity of different styles as well as different stages of development of the same style within a given epoch and within a narrower or wider geographical area. Cf. H. Focillon, *La Vie des Formes* (Paris, 1934); English translation, "The Life of Forms in Art" (New York: 1948). The fact, however, that all these different styles (individual style, school style, material style) either lack a common denominator which allows their differentiations and makes them understandable or that such a common denominator ("period style," "national style," "ethnic" style) must be formulated so abstractly that it no longer states anything on the concrete works of art is a consequence of the same presupposition.

Instead of a theoretical discussion two examples will briefly illustrate that this assumption is untenable.

The concept of the "archaic" or "primitive" (as well as that of "classical," "Baroque," or "Romantic," etc.), as is known, today no longer serves exclusively or even primarily to designate a particular stylistic stage within historical development. Rather, it is defined, even by the exponents of an "immanent" history of art, as the common denominator of specific world views to which specific formal characteristics in works of art stemming from entirely different periods correspond: the archaic conceptual image ("intellectual realism") reveals, in contradistinction to the classical perceptual image ("optical realism," W. Deonna), man's physical, spiritual, and social dependency, his anonymity, the mightiness of the world of matter.

Thus the "Hera of Samos" (Louvre, ca. 570-560 B.C., fig. 10) and the statues of the Royal Portal of Chartres (ca. 1145-70, fig.11) are generally considered as an artistic expression of the same "archaic" world view. Again, in the twentieth century, the same expression is embodied in a work like Brancusi's "The Kiss" (1908, fig. 12). Assuming that all characterizations in terms of form and content of the archaic as a historically constant (though not continuous) world view were accepted, does it follow that this same world view actually expresses— even in the three aforementioned works—the same (positive or negative, objective or subjective, etc.) relation between man and the spiritual and material world environing him?

Conversely, cannot works which are formally utterly different from each other invoke and convey feelings about life, world views, and mental attitudes which from the point of view of philosophy, sociology of knowledge, and religion represent the same "type"?

The works of de Chirico and Munch are certainly fundamentally different from each other in their form, composition, and subject matter, whereas Toulouse-Lautrec and Munch are closely related as exponents of "art nouveau." Nevertheless, the works of these two latter artists (who are of the same age) exhibit a marked contrast in terms of their expressive content. Compare, for example, Toulouse-Lautrec's "At the Moulin Rouge: La Goulue and her Sister," 1892 (fig. 13) with Munch's "Anxiety," painting, 1894; lithograph, 1896 (fig. 14). On the other hand, many works of Munch parallel the early de Chirico in their conception of the relation of man to man, man to nature, man to the

10. *Hera of Samos* [Photographie Giraudon, Paris]

11. Statues of the Royal Portal of Chartres [Photo-
graphie Giraudon, Paris]

12. *The Kiss* by Brancusi [Philadelphia Museum of Art,
The Louis and Walter Arensberg Collection]

13. *At the Moulin Rouge: La Goulue and Her Sister*,
a color lithograph by Toulouse-Lautrec [Collection,
The Museum of Modern Art, New York. Gift of
Abby Aldrich Rockefeller]

14.  *Anxiety*, a color lithograph by Munich [Collection, The Museum of Modern Art, New York]

environing world: employing totally different artistic means both painters show the inner or external, spiritual or physical isolation and loneliness of man, his individuality reduced to a masklike or shadowlike appearance.[11] Compare Munch's "Anxiety" with de Chirico's "The Nostalgia of the Infinite," 1913-14 (?), (fig. 15).

Thus the comparison of the expressive content of the works of Toulouse-Lautrec, Munch, and de Chirico refutes the assertion that the formal similarity of works of art perforce guarantees the similarity or sameness of the world views that are expressed in them. But this does not necessarily hold true for the three archaic works. For the concept of expressive content *alone* does not suffice to answer the question that has been posed: whether under changed historical conditions the "constant" of world views embraces, or can embrace, in each case an entirely different, or even contrary, (social) meaning.

A comparative analysis of the aforementioned works would, of course, show the much greater differentiation of the human body in the Greek and Gothic statues as compared to Brancusi's "The Kiss," the much greater emphasis marking the tensed unity which binds and separates man and matter. But only when the results of this "immanent" sociology are complemented by and combined with the results of general sociological investigations does it become possible to understand the expressive content of the Greek and Gothic sculptures as embodiments of an active attitude of man toward his environment, a struggle for his spiritual and physical independence (individuation). Whereas the almost absolute sway of matter, or of a being dominated by matter so persuasively presented by the modern artist, expresses a passive acceptance of existing conditions, even when the minimal distinction made between man and stone subjectively is "meant" to signify the dream or wish for a return to a lost elemental unity.[12]

11. Obviously these remarks do not exhaust the expressive content of the works; they are intended only to indicate the similarity of their fundamental attitude. See also de Chirico's "Melancholy and Mystery of a Street," 1914, and Munch's "The Scream," painting, 1893; lithograph, 1895.

12. The question whether and in what sense Brancusi's work is to be considered a "purely private" statement or as a superindividual, "typical" artistic expression of the early twentieth century, reflecting the real (moral, material, spiritual) helplessness of the individual within the society of his time, cannot be investigated here. At all events, the question cannot be answered without comparing at least the whole of Brancusi's work, not

15. *The Nostalgia of the Infinite* by de Chirico [Collection, The Museum of Modern Art, New York]

In other words, only in connection with general sociology is it possible to determine which specific (though always complex) sociological signification the world view conveyed by a work of art possesses within the historical situation as a whole (expressed in catchwords, "world-affirming" or "world-withdrawing," "revolutionary" or "reactionary," "realistic," "idealizing," or "idealistic").

This statement by no means signifies that ultimately what presumably was "read" from the work on the basis of its visual data is now "read into" it from the outside. Rather, it confirms the methodological and empirical claims to validity made for the concept of expressive content in the course of the preceding reflections. For, as the analyses of the paintings have shown, the potential content does not refer to single historical facts but only and always to the *general* social structure of the period in which the work originated. This structure can be recognized precisely because the potential content reveals that the ideological contents and attitudes formulated in the work are not the expression of the "whole" society but the expression of the groups or strata of the period—in each case different—culturally, economically, or religiously dominant.

In this way the concept of the "style of a period" acquires a concrete content whose possibility of differentiation is limited only by the number of the extant works of art of the same date. For in contradistinction to the pure history of styles, the expressive content makes it possible to understand their "formal" differences as differences in world views stemming from the same historical reality.

---

simply this one piece of sculpture, with the production of his immediate contemporaries. This problem will be examined in a separate work along with a discussion of modern art in terms of expressive content.

# 7.

# *The Artist and the Public*

At this time [1311] the altarpiece for the high altar was finished . . . which is far more beautiful and devout and larger [than the old one], and it is painted on the back with stories of the Old and New Testament. And on the day that it was carried to the Duomo the shops were shut, and the bishop conducted a great and devout company of priests and friars in solemn procession, accompanied by the nine signiors, and all the officers of the commune, and all the people, and one after another the worthiest with lighted candles in their hands took places near the picture, and behind came the women and children with great devotion. And they accompanied the said picture up to the Duomo, making the procession around the Campo, as is the custom, all the bells ringing joyously, out of reverence for so noble a picture as this.[1]

*A pitiful poor woman, shrunk and old,*
  *I am, and nothing learn'd in letter-lore:*
*Within my parish-cloister I behold*
  *A painted Heaven where harps and lutes adore,*
  *And eke a Hell whose damned folk seethe full sore:*
*One bringeth fear, the other joy to me.*
*That joy, great Goddess, make thou mine to be—*
  *Thou of whom all must ask it, even as I;*
*And that which faith desires, that let it see.*
  *For in this faith I choose to live and die.*[2]

1. Translation by Charles Eliot Norton, quoted in Elizabeth G. Holt, *A Documentary History of Art*, vol. I (Doubleday Anchor, 1947) p. 135.
2. From "The Ballade To Our Lady" by Francois Villon, translated by Dante Gabriel Rossetti in *Francois Villon* by D. B. Wyndham Lewis (New York, 1928) p. 345.

*I beg you, of that motley crowd cease telling*
*At sight of whom the spirit takes to flight!*
*. . . Reflect! You have a tender wood to split;*
*And those for whom you write, just see!*
*If this one's driven hither by ennui,*
*Another leaves a banquet sated with its vapours;*
*And—what the very worst will always be—*
*Many come fresh from reading magazines and papers.*
*Men haste distraught to us as to the masquerade,*
*And every step but winged by curiousity;*
*The ladies give a treat, all in their best arrayed,*
*And play their part without a fee.*
*. . . Observe the patrons near at hand!*
*They are half cold, half coarse are they.*[3]

The revue was a clever and amusing one, but it also had a stylish quality of fashionable smartness that was more and more beginning to mark the productions of the theatre and the responses of the audience. . . . The revue was one of those productions which people were beginning to "wear" as they "wore" books or plays or a dress: people went to the revue more because it was "the thing to do," the thing that every one was talking about, than because they had a genuine desire to go, more because they had been told that it was "amusing" than from any deep conviction that they would find it so.[4]

What is at issue in all these utterances, so different in terms of content and of time? It is always the same and yet not the same issue, namely, that link in the relationship between art and society—in *every* art and *every* society—that is absolutely indispensable: the public.

But what is "the public"? What Valéry said of nature is also true of the public: the public, this myth . . .

At all events, "the" public is an abstraction. Historically, there

3. J. W. von Goethe, *Faust*, Part 1, Prelude on the Stage, translated by George Madison Priest, *Faust Parts One and Two* (New York: Knopf, 1967) pp. 5 and 7.

4. Thomas Wolfe, *Of Time and the River* (New York: Scribner's, 1935) p. 503.

is no public given once and for all; there are only strata, groups, and individuals within a particular society, which in each case constitute more or less numerous, differentiated, localized, articulated, active or passive, and important segments of the public interested in various fields of art. In other words, the public is a socio-historical category and what at any given time in any given society is understood by the concept "public," how it is constituted, whether or not it views itself as a "public" or is thus viewed by the artist, are all questions subject to historically changing conditions.

Thus it is impossible to make statements about the public in general valid for all historical periods. But, on the other hand, it is equally impossible to discuss works of art and artists without positing some kind of a public. For both the concept of the work of art and of the artist are inconceivable without a public. Perhaps Charles Lalo's definition of the socially conditioned nature of the extraordinary individual, although it does not specifically refer to the work of art and its audience, demonstrates best of all the indissoluble bond between works of art and publics: "The exceptional character of a great man consists primarily in his ability to express certain social needs with exceptional intensity. In default of which, without success and without an audience, that is, without value in the known world, he would be but a negligible exception, as an individual case of insanity."[5]

Applied to the work of art and the artist, it by no means follows from these statements that every work of art at the time of its origin necessarily has a public that recognizes the artist as "artist" and certain objects as "works of art." If so, entire epochs which to present-day man represent artistic high points would have to be stricken from the history of art.

But before attempting the investigation of some of the complicated problems which the relationship of artist and public presents in every age, although differently in every age, it is important to emphasize one fact: namely, "today's" public—that is, the people who are more or less interested in art, who visit museums, go to exhibitions,

5. Charles Lalo, *Notions d'Esthétique* (Paris: Alcan, 1925) p. 69: "Le caractère d'exception d'un grand homme est surtout d'exprimer avec une intensité exceptionelle certains besoins sociaux. Faute de quoi, sans succès et sans public, c. à. d. sans valeur dans aucune conscience connue, il ne serait qu'exception négligeable comme c'est un cas de folie individuel."

and buy paintings, sculptures, or reproductions (without thereby being "collectors")—this public forgets that "artists" have not existed in all periods and that therefore a public in the modern sense of the word did not exist either.

The word "artiste" in its modern meaning was not included in the dictionary of the illustrious *Académie Française* until 1762. And as for the public, Erich Auerbach's investigations, for example, show that in France the word was first used in 1629, in its particular application to the theater audience.[6] What is true of the theater audience, of course, does not necessarily apply to the audience of the fine arts in general and painting in particular; what is true of France and specifically Paris in the seventeenth century is not necessarily applicable to Rome, Venice, London, Amsterdam, or Madrid in the same period.[7] Accordingly the one thing that is clear is that all generalizations about artists and their public are without scientific value or, at best, half-truths only. Nevertheless, such a generalization will serve here as point of departure in order to clarify the problem.

The extraordinary ambivalence toward artists that in one way or another characterizes the basic attitude of every average member of the modern public is a modern attitude that may not be mechanically applied to the past. It has nothing to do, for example, with Plato's passionate polemic against poets and bards, who by their very nature endanger society; for him the practitioners of the "fine arts" are not yet "artists." The typically modern attitude, as passionless as it is ambivalent, can be characterized roughly as follows: on the one hand, every layman who is interested in art is inclined to honor the artist as a sort of higher being, and he willingly submits to the spell that surrounds all genuine creativity. On the other hand, he has, at the same time and especially toward living artists a feeling bordering on conviction that they are not to be taken seriously, viewing them as arrogant, unreliable, frivolous, with all the clichés of bohemian life—in short, everything which contradicts the "seriousness of life" and re-

6. Erich Auerbach, *Untersuchungen zur Geschichte der franzoesischen Bildung, La Cour et la Ville* (Berne: 1951) pp. 12–50.
7. On this point see the extremely interesting and excellently documented book by Francis Haskell, *Patrons and Painters: A Study in the Relations Between Italian Art and Society in the Age of the Baroque* (New York: Knopf, 1963).

sponsibility in the sense of the solid merchant, the conscientious craftsman, the civil-servant and skilled worker. (This ambivalence, in a typical form, permeates the work of the *bourgeois manqué* Thomas Mann
to the end of his life. The same attitude is expressed in a banal and
everyday form in the fact that even today parents, with all their
vaunted respect for creativity, are not exactly overjoyed if their daughter wants to marry a—not yet famous!—painter or sculptor.)

A similar ambivalence marks the attitude of the artist: on
the one hand, a deep contempt for the philistine, the uncomprehending shopkeeper; on the other—and not indeed because as the German
saying has it, "art cries out for bread"—the touching and obstinate
faith that some day he will be understood by the "public."[8]

Whatever the reasons for this modern relation between artist
and public and whoever may be "guilty" for its negative aspects—the
public accuses the artists and the artists the public—every "average"
member of the public takes it for granted that artists have existed at all
times. And if the correctness of his assumption were questioned, he
would cite the cave paintings of Lascaux and Altamira, the names of
Phidias and Apelles, the anonymous masters of the cathedral sculpture
of the Middle Ages, and other famous artists of the past. Similarly, the
modern artist assumes as a matter of course that there has always been
a public throughout history. In fact, the modern artist is particularly
prone to contrast the contemporary public with an ideal public of the
past—that is, with a public with "true" understanding of art—people
who *by their artistic comprehension* encouraged the work of those
masters of past epochs whose works are particularly admired by modern
artists.

As has already been indicated, both of these assumptions do
not accord with the facts. Obviously the sculptors of the archaic Greek
statuary, the painters of Romanesque frescoes, etc., were artists in the
modern sense of the word. In the minds of their contemporaries, however, that is, of their public, they were not "artists" at all but rather

8. There is no need to consider the silly attitude exhibited by
some contemporary artists, who purport to see in public appreciation a proof
that their work is bad, although this attitude is sociologically, if not artistically, interesting. That it is only a pose is shown very clearly by the fact that
these artists do not destroy the works which public approval has shown to
be bad!

artisans. And as such they were incorporated into and lumped together with all those who practiced a trade in the *artes mecanicae* as against the *artes liberales*. Neither architecture nor painting nor sculpture belonged to the *artes liberales*, the "free arts."[9] True, architects, viewed socially, were the first to rise from their rank as practitioners of a "mechanical" art to the social position of a "free" profession or to the circles of "educated" society in general. Nevertheless, it should make us pause when a theoretician and architect of genius of the early Renaissance such as Leon Battista Alberti still takes great care to avoid being considered as a professional architect who is paid for his work. Similarly, there are good grounds for Leonardo's recurrent and insistent assertion that painting is a *cosa mentale*, something mental —namely, the effort to free the painter from the stigma of being a craftsman of the mechanical arts. The same basic attitude, this sharp cleavage between manual laborers and "free" men who do not have to work with their hands to earn their living, whereby manual labor is contemptuously attributed only to slaves or other people who "do not belong to the cream of society," also finds expression in the famous and oft-cited utterance of antiquity: "Everyone admires the Zeus of Phidias, but who would want to be Phidias?"[10]

This quotation, however, is not to be understood as suggesting that the lower social position of the artisan is the *only* explanation

9. In connection with this point and what follows, see especially A. Dresdner, *Die Entstehung der Kunstkritik im Zusammenhang der Geschichte des europaeischen Kunstlebens* (Munich: 1913) vol. I; E. Zilsel, *Die Entstehung des Geniebegriffs, ein Beitrag zur Ideengeschichte der Antike und des Fruehkapitalismus* (Tuebingen, 1926); B. Schweitzer, *Der bildende Kuenstler und der Begriff des Kuenstlerischen in der Antike. Neue Heidelberger Jahrbuecher* (N.F., 1925); M. Wackernagel, *Der Lebensraum des Kuenstlers in der florentinischen Renaissance* (Leipzig: 1938); H. Huth, *Kuenstler und Werkstatt der Spaetgotik* (Augsburg: 1923); N. Pevsner, *Academies of Art: Past and Present* (Cambridge, 1940); P. Kristeller, "The Modern System of the Arts: A Study in the History of Aesthetics," *Journal of the History of Ideas* (Oct. 12, 1951, and Jan. 13, 1952); R. Krautheimer and T. Krautheimer-Hess, *Lorenzo Ghiberti* (Princeton University Press, 1956) especially chapter XIX, "Humanists and Artists," pp. 294–305; A. Hauser, *Philosophie der Kunstgeschichte* (Munich: 1958); C. Curtius, "Zum antiken Kuenstlerbild," in B. Schweitzer, *Zur Kunst der Antike* (Tuebingen, 1963) vol. I; Previtali, *op. cit.*, pp. 44–46.

10. Cf. Pauly's *Real-Encyclopaedie der klassischen Altertumswissenschaft*, revised ed., 1938. "The Zeus was certainly greatly admired by the contemporaries of Phidias; although we have no testimony to this effect."

for the distinction between the work admired and its creator. Other factors, to be discussed later, also play a role. The stigma attached to the wage-earner in antiquity, nevertheless, is clearly apparent in Philip of Macedonia's harsh criticism of his son Alexander on the occasion when the latter played the flute with a flawless perfection at a banquet: "Aren't you ashamed to play so well?" (That is, like a professional.)[11] And this at a period which already was indulging in a certain type of genius-worship which was also extended to practitioners of the fine arts.

But is not the question whether ancient Greece, the Middle Ages and even the periods after the Renaissance considered artists as artists in the modern sense or as artisans, wage-earners, and "subjects" completely irrelevant? Is not the only important thing the fact that artists created works of art which offer the contemporary viewer an artistic experience, regardless of the respect or lack of respect accorded to their creators? Furthermore, if it be true, as was asserted earlier, that in most periods of known history there not only were no "artists" but also no public in the modern sense, would it not be logical to assume that there also were no "works of art"? This, of course, seems to be the height of absurdity. Would all the distinctions between the work of art, the artist, and the public, especially the question of the indissoluble bond between them, be but futile hairsplitting, which could contribute nothing to the explanation of works of art or to the understanding of creative artists and just as little to the understanding of the relationship between art and society?

No. The distinctions are justified, and the question of the relevancy of the ancient Greek or the Renaissance attitude toward the artist is not rhetorical, because content, form, function—in short, the concepts of art and of the work of art—were and *are* dependent to the highest degree on the social value that is attributed to the position and the work of the artist.[12] For these conceptions prevailing within a society fundamentally determine the relationship between artist and pub-

---

11. Xenophon, *Memorabilia* 4, 7. Quoted in A. Dresdner, *op. cit.*
12. Karl Mannheim formulates this as follows: "It seems, however, to be a sociological principle that the social value of intellectual culture is a function of the social status of those who produce it." In *Mensch und Gesellschaft im Zeitalter des Umbaus* (Leyden: 1935) p. 77; English translation, *Man and Society in an Age of Reconstruction* (London, 1950).

lic and between public and work of art and, consequently, the whole complex of questions which today is subsumed under art appreciation and art criticism.

Indeed, the apparently paradoxical statement that no "works of art" were created during the greater part of known history is not at all absurd. Rather, it provides insights into the "necessity of art"[13] that can be acquired neither by purely empirical nor purely logical approaches to the question. From the historical point of view, further, it should be pointed out that before the second half of the nineteenth century, save for some isolated instances, there were no "works of art" and no "paintings" in the modern sense of the term, namely, the work of art as an object of so-called purely aesthetic enjoyment for the individual beholder or, on the part of the artist, as an object embodying the most personal expression of his deepest experiences.

On the basis of this currently accepted definition Malraux is quite right in saying that, strictly speaking, works of art exist as "works of art" in museums only although—or precisely because— they lose in the modern museum (an invention of the nineteenth century!) both their meaning and their function. In a museum, for example, a portrait is not primarily the image of a particular person; an illuminated book of hours is no longer a prayer book and a calendar, and a black- or red-figured amphora no longer primarily a vessel for wine. If a beholder is charmed by this amphora, it is not because he recognizes in its decoration the ecstatic procession of Dionysus. And if he remains indifferent, it is not because he no longer believes in the dangerous power of this god. In other words, the average member of today's public enjoys the works in terms of their "formal values" and of the mood they evoke in him. Whereas the work's particular religious, political, or mythological meaning and original purpose are disregarded to an extreme degree.

As previously shown,[14] the artistic content of a work can certainly be grasped independently of its particular meaning. Indeed, precisely this fact makes it possible to prove the existence of artistic quality in a work. However, this does *not* signify that the original

13. The title of a book by Ernst Fischer (Dresden: Verlag der Kunst, 1959).

14. See Chapter 2.

meaning of the work was marginal to its creation and of no importance to the public of the time. On the contrary, the thematic meaning was familiar to the contemporary public as a matter of course. Moreover, meaning and subject matter, over the millenia, constituted the external occasion of the creation of the work. Thus the meaning was binding upon the artist and often determined his representation even in minute details.[15] The so-called free creative artist who chooses (or must choose?) his themes and their treatment by himself is a phenomenon of the modern period, even though occasional examples of free choice or free treatment of themes by the artist can be found as early as the second half of the sixteenth century.

The fact that in the past the public understood its contemporary works in terms of their meaning and subject matter is of great importance because this familiarity provided a secure basis for general criteria of critical evaluation: a criticism based on criteria which the artist could and did accept although (or precisely because) it had absolutely nothing to do with "art criticism" in the modern sense of the word.[16]

Hence, an apparent paradox ensues, namely, that a criticism of art understandable to both public and artists seems to be possible at a moment in time, and perhaps *only* then, when the criteria underlying this criticism are extra-artistic. That is, when they deal with questions concerning the subject matter and function of the work and *not* with those which are of particular concern to modern art criticism: originality, color, form, composition, etc.

This statement may appear simple, which it is not, inasmuch as agreement on the theme and function of the work of art posits a more or less homogeneous public. But what is a homogeneous public? The simplest answer seems to be: a public that shares common interests. Do thousands of spectators at a boxing match or a football game therefore constitute a homogeneous public? Obviously not, and not only because interest in art is held to be a somewhat "higher" or more "spiritual" interest than interest in sports. Rather, the crowd that gath-

---

15. Apart from other evidence, contracts that demonstrate this satisfactorily have been preserved.

16. Cf. Wind's remarks on Michelangelo's reaction to the "interference" of Clement VII in the execution of the Medici chapel: E. Wind, *Art and Anarchy* (London: 1963) p. 92.

ers at a sports event lacks a unifying factor which binds its members beyond their more or less short-term common interest; namely, a common scale of values.

Using the concept of a common scale of values as a point of departure, a genuine public would then consist of people whose essential interests are determined by the same, or at least by basically similar, values. The question of what constitutes the basis of such similarly oriented values or the factors conditioning them—common religion, membership in the same social class, class-consciousness, common profession, etc.—can be left open.

Even the greatest concordance regarding "life-ideals," however, obviously does not exclude individual differences in psychological types, temperaments, artistic talents, and inclinations. But it is just as obvious that the interests, ideals, and ideologies which at any given time prevail within a society or a social group powerfully influence the *evaluation* of these differences in temperaments, types, and talents. A society, for example, for which novelty, individuality, and originality constitute the highest values in all fields will judge works of art from entirely different points of view than a society whose highest ideals are geared to the preservation of tradition, of the patrimony and the customs of the past. An artist who, in a society dedicated to the cult of originality and individuality, created works that are as similar as possible to those of his predecessors in themes, composition, types, color, etc., would be viewed as a feeble epigone at best, but more likely dismissed as a plagiarist or a non-artist. Conversely, an artist who, in a society dedicated to tradition and the norms handed down from the past, dared to create at a certain period of the Middle Ages a work marked by innovations, such as representing an earthly figure with the same dimensions as a heavenly one—so rash a person would at best be viewed as insane, if not as a heretic, with all the ensuing consequences.[17] Although it is true that a homogeneous public shares essen-

17. Although factually correct, the example is misleading in this simplified form. For not only are notions of (artistic) originality, individuality, etc., historical notions which are not defined in the same way, either in different periods or by different social strata within the same society, but the historically given societies or cultural communities likewise have utterly different tolerance thresholds for groups and individuals who deviate from the generally sanctioned conventions, norms, and institutionalized types of behavior. Cf. Ruth Benedict, *Patterns of Culture* (Pelican Books, 1946) original

tially similar interests, it must be borne in mind that hardly any society exists which in its totality constitutes a *single* homogeneous public. Every developed society encompasses more or less differentiated strata of publics and, above all, strata which, albeit homogeneous in themselves, oppose each other. In other words, the fact that people are contemporaries—even if they belong to the same generation—does not necessarily unify them as a homogeneous public.

The story is told that near the end of his reign Louis XIV, at the sight of Dutch seventeenth-century genre pictures, indignantly ordered the removal of "those monstrosities" from the royal chambers. This reaction proves neither that the Sun King had no understanding of art nor that the middle class, which loved genre paintings, was imbued with the most refined artistic understanding in contrast to His Majesty. The opposite reactions show only that both Louis XIV and the contemporary middle class judged works of art in terms of extra-artistic criteria stemming from fundamentally different and opposing sets of val-

---

ed. 1934; Robert L. Lynd and Helen M. Lynd, *Middletown in Transition: A Study in Cultural Conflict* (New York: 1937) p. 448, footnote 46. Here only a brief allusion can be made to the importance which the social preference or rejection of certain fields of art and of *certain types of artists* has with respect to the so-called "generation problem," that is, the appearance or absence of certain talents within the course of art history. All kinds of extra-artistic reasons may condition this preference or rejection of certain types of artists. It should be pointed out, however, that types of artists, Focillon's "families of minds," are by definition wholly different from the typology of the psychologists.

Tiepolo's genius is certainly not explained by the fact that the old Venetian noble families attached all the more value to seeing their former importance glorified as their international influence (political, economic, etc.) decreased. The particular character of his genius certainly aroused the need for his art as much as it gratified it. And yet there should be no underestimation of the fact that "for Tiepolo, as for so many Venetian artists, the final break with the heavy style of the seventeenth century did not—perhaps could not—come in his native city, so conservative in temper." (Haskell, *op. cit.*, p. 253 ff., as well as the whole analysis of the Venetian artistic milieu in the eighteenth century in part III.) In other words, a whole generation of mediocre, excellent, or brilliant painters of still lifes, genre scenes, portraits, etc., no more suddenly springs into being than does a generation of artists with predominantly lyrical, monumental, intellectual, or sensuous talents. Rather, the needs of various social groups or of relatively undifferentiated societies at any particular time foster or hinder the various creative abilities and thus influence the selection of the artistic types which predominate in any given period.

ues. The king found the subject matter of the paintings—perhaps a couple of peasants in a tavern or a cook at work in the kitchen—below his dignity. He viewed them as a personal insult and thus was unable to recognize their "purely artistic value." Or, in other words, the king refused to separate artistic enjoyment from the totality of his social and private existence and experience. No doubt the possibility of such a separation no more crossed his mind than it did the minds of his bourgeois subjects.[18] By this attitude the king and the middle-class audience attest that they were far more responsive to and aware of the impact of art and of the importance of its function than are twentieth-century connoisseurs who pride themselves on their "pure" understanding of art.

This does not signify, naturally, that people of past periods paid no attention to the "artistic" aspects of works of art. Of course, it is difficult, or even impossible, to determine whether and to what extent Villon's mother found the figures in Paradise "beautiful" and the devils and sinners in Hell "ugly." Did the heavenly figures seem "beautiful" to her, perhaps, only because she knew that the picture was a representation of Paradise? Or did she, as a matter of course, understand the portrayal to be of Paradise because the figures were "beautiful"? Whatever the answer, for the poor woman who could neither read nor write the "artistic" aspect of the picture was at all events inseparable from its theme and meaning, precisely because the theme and meaning were understood as values corresponding to her own integrated image of the world, no matter how limited it may have been.

But even for beholders whose cultural level is indisputable and who were fully equipped consciously to make the distinction between the "artistic" and the philosophical aspects of a work of art, the evaluation of the work was still anchored in extra-artistic criteria.

Hans Fugger, for example, who in 1568 had commissioned a Resurrection for the St. Moritz church in Augsburg, writes: "But the Resurrection is not done as it should have been, for our Lord should be rising from the grave and not be represented as flying ... therefore I

---

18. G. Reitlinger, *The Economics of Taste: The Rise and Fall of Picture Prices, 1760–1960* (London: 1961) p. 12: "Opinions are divided in assigning the origins of the Dutch picture cult to the prudery of Mme. de Maintenon, who disliked nudes about the place, or to the attractive loot that became available when Louis XIV's forces invaded the Netherlands."

don't know whether he [the painter] will do for me or not. From the outside one would think that it was an angel and not Christ himself who is floating in the air. . . . So this altar-canvas or *quadro* does not seem suitable (for it is too much *à la italiana,* impious and of such a kind that the person standing in front of the altar does not know how it is intended)."

And after a Trinity had been ordered in place of the Resurrection, he writes: "I would like it to be devout and beautiful and not such that the painter is displaying his art only and nothing more behind it . . .[19] but by all means I would like to see a small sketch or layout beforehand, so that the result won't be like adding apples and pears." And finally, upon sending to Italy for a *"disegno,"* once more he emphasized: ". . . but I would like him not only to possess great art but also to be very devout. Your Italian painters are too *vagi.*"[20]

The two examples, which could be continued at length, suffice to show that the different public in each case possessed a criterion for its evaluation of art even if—to emphasize the point once more—this evaluation is not at all "art criticism" according to present-day concepts. But how the artists themselves reacted to this type of criticism has remained open so far.

The simplest way to answer this question, perhaps, is by pointing out that there practically were no unrecognized geniuses before the beginning of the nineteenth century (despite the Rembrandt legend, which indeed it is).[21] This may seem to be a very superficial answer. But this "prosaic" statement, which says nothing about the psychology of the artist, the problem of the creative process, or the romantic conflict between artist and public, thereby substantiates the

19. Strange to say, Hebbel uses almost the same expressions in his *Agnes Bernauer,* Act 3, Scene 4.

20. Quoted in F. Wuertemberger, *Der Manierismus* (Vienna-Munich: 1961) p. 111. Cf. Georg Lill, *Hans Fugger (1531–1598) und die Kunst. Ein Beitrag zur Geschichte der Spaetrenaissance in Sueddeutschland* (Leipzig: 1908) pp. 30 ff. and 132. Fugger uses the idiomatic expression "damit es keinen Matthäus zur Fastnacht abgebe" here rendered by "like adding apples and pears." (St. Mathew's Day is September 21 and thus can never coincide with "Fassnacht," that is, carnival). The word *vagi* at the end of the quote has multiple meanings, such as a lack of modesty or "decorum," or lack of preciseness or clarity.

21. Seymour Slive, *Rembrandt and his Critics, 1630–1730* (The Hague: 1953).

fact of the absence of this conflict. Naturally this does not signify that before the beginning of the nineteenth-century painters and sculptors had no artistic problems (in contradistinction to problems of content and technique). But because the artists understood, if not shared, the social ideals and goals of their public, it was possible and natural for them (no matter how far they stepped beyond this limitation in their works) to fuse their specific artistic problems with the representation of the ideological values of the different strata of publics in terms of subject matter and meaning.

In short, artists and works of art had their specific function and position *within*, not outside, the social structure. They worked for patrons with whom they were often personally acquainted or at least they knew the social circles for which they were working, whether or not they themselves belonged to those circles. Naturally, even before the nineteenth century there were poor artists just as in all occupations there were some who earned a lot and others who earned little. But there was no theory contending that being poor and living in misery were a requisite, or even a precondition, to prove the vocation of a genuine artist. This theory originated and could only have originated in the nineteenth century as a correlate of the modern notion of the "misunderstood" genius. The present-day concept of genius is primarily characterized by the fact that it opposes the genius to the mass and that in the genius capability for achievement rather than the achievement as such is admired as a special and inexplicable gift.[22] The opposition between mass and genius is logically and historically prior to the concept of the misunderstood genius. But how did this opposition, unknown before the end of the eighteenth century (with respect to the fine arts), arise and why did it sharpen into the concept of the *necessarily* "misunderstood" genius in the course of the nineteenth century?

This opposition generally is explained by the new structure of the public which, since the end of the French Revolution, was now based on the upper and middle strata of the new bourgeois-capitalist industrial society (although at entirely different tempi and in different groupings in different countries). That this new bourgeois public had no artistic tradition of its own; that the old social bonds of the *ancien régime* had lost their force, drying up many resources of employment

22. Cf. Zilsel, *op. cit.*

for the artist; that machine-produced goods destroyed the sense of quality and beauty; that the transformation of the *citoyen* into the bourgeois engendered distrust of "revolutionary" artistic innovations; that the anonymous market entailed an anonymous public; and that all these and other economic, technical, and political factors necessarily conduced to an alienation between artist and public inevitably appear at some point or other in every manual dealing with nineteenth-century painting.

All these familiar explanations are indeed correct. They neglect, however, the fact that the alienation of artist and public is but a special aspect of a broader alienation—of the self-alienation to which all are subjected, with a greater intensity than ever before, in the new capitalist society.

> If the community makes function the measure of a man, when it respects in one of its citizens only memory, in another a tabulating intellect, in a third only mechanical skill; if, indifferent to character, it here lays stress upon knowledge alone, and there pardons the profoundest darkness of the intellect so long as it co-exists with a spirit of order and a law-abiding demeanour—if at the same time it requires these special aptitudes to be exercised with an intensity proportionate to the loss of extension which it permits in the individuals concerned—can we then wonder that the remaining aptitudes of the mind become neglected in order to bestow every attention upon the only one which brings in honour and profit? We know indeed that vigorous genius does not make the boundaries of its concern the boundaries of its activity; but mediocre talent consumes the whole meagre sum of its strength in the concern that falls to its lot, and it must be no ordinary head that has something left over for private pursuits without prejudice to its vocation . . . and so gradually individual concrete life is extinguished, in order that the abstract life of the whole may prolong its sorry existence. . . .[23]

23. Friedrich von Schiller, *On the Aesthetic Education of Man*, translated by Reginald Snell (London: Routledge and Kegan Paul, 1954) 6th letter.

In this connection it is interesting to observe that the problem of general human self-alienation, as described by Schiller in 1795, in its particular consequences for the situation of the plastic artists was already being dealt with in the novel and the drama at the same time, that is, about fifty years before the art critics, economists, and sociologists of the nineteenth century tackled it. The artist in opposition to the masses, to life or to reality appears already in Heinse's *Ardinghello* (1787). This work ushers in the fast-growing series of artist-protagonists who must sacrifice either their art to life or their life to art, since the conflict has become unbridgeable, however differently the various authors motivate it. Consider, for example, Tieck's *Sternbald*, Balzac's Frenhofer (in *Le Chef-d'oeuvre Inconnu*), or Ibsen's Rubeck (in *When We Dead Awaken*).[24]

In other words, even before the alienation of artist and public was imprinted on the general consciousness as something "typical" or "self-evident," the new special position of the artist and his work was recognized as a tragic fact of life by poets and writers.

In the new capitalist world the artist and his work lost their former clearly defined position and function within the social structure. Subjectively and objectively artists and their works became outsiders. This new state of affairs is most strikingly revealed in the fact

24. For summaries of the portrayal of the artist in literature, see, for example, H. W. Keim, "Der Maler im Roman," *Literarisches Echo*, vol. 2 (1918–19); Karl Helbling, *Die Gestalt des Kuenstlers in der neueren Dichtung* (Berne: 1922); H. Heckel, *Das Bild des Kuenstlers im neueren deutschen Roman*, "Festschrift fuer Koch" (Breslau: 1926); Kaete Laserstein, *Die Gestalt des bildenden Kuenstlers in der Dichtung, Stoff und Motivgeschichte der deutschen Literatur*, No. 12 (1931); R. S. Collins, *The Artist in Modern German Drama*, Baltimore, 1940 (doctoral thesis); A. Ponceau, *Balzac et les Peintres*, "Revue d'Esthétique," tome XI, fasc. 1 & 2, (January–June, 1958). In this connection it is also important to note that in American literature the plastic artist almost never appears as a hero; rather, it is the writer or journalist who appears as the typical representative of the "creative" man. In a completely different context, and without differentiating between the practitioner of the fine arts and the literary artist, Henry A. Murray states, "For example, a sociological factor which can hardly be overlooked in accounting for the prevalence of the Orpheus or Ishmael theme in American literature is the generally low status, the widespread neglect and belittlement of the artist in our culture." In *Personality and Creative Imagination*, English Institute Annual, 1942, (New York: Columbia University Press, 1943) pp. 155–6. There is no reason to deny the validity of this statement with respect to the current situation in American literature as well.

that never in the course of history has there been a public which, as a whole, so vigorously rejected and so uncomprehendingly or inimically opposed the art of its own time as did the public of the second half of the nineteenth century in France—not to mention other artistically less developed countries. That in 1863 Napoleon III himself ordered the opening of the famous "Salon des Refusés" was not the result of pressure from the most influential (and the richest) strata within the public but of the protests of the younger generation of artists and the small circle of their admirers, for the most part themselves artists and writers. In short, "intellectuals" and "outsiders" whose admiration increased rather than diluted the distrust or the resistance of the "official" circles to the "new" artists. Thus the "Salon des Refusés" represents more than just another example of the usual intrigues and petty jealousies among the members of the jury and the artists. Rather, it attests that the separation between "official" and "living" art, between the contemporary artist and his contemporary public, had become a social and cultural fact characterizing the situation of artist and art in modern bourgeois society of the nineteenth century. This basic situation still exists today despite enormously important differences which will be discussed later.

But what distinguished "official" painting, whose representatives (their names for the most part are known today only to specialists) received government and private commissions, honors, and high prices, from the new rejected art of the Barbizon painters, of Courbet, of Manet, Monet, Renoir, Gauguin, etc.—in short, from the painting of all the artists whose works, in the eyes of the modern public, attest to the glory of nineteenth-century French painting? Does this distinction lend itself to generalization? For it is simply not true that all the "official" and recognized painters were bad and all the artists attacked by the press and the general public, excellent. The distinction is discernible not only in the attitude of the public toward its contemporary painters but also in the judgments it passed on Old Masters. Thus, for example, in 1840 the National Gallery in London paid 330 pounds sterling for Van Eyck's (today) "priceless" "Giovanni Arnolfini and His Bride," but 600 pounds for Guido Reni's "Lot and his Daughters." A hundred years later the "market value" of the Van Eyck painting was a thousand times as great while the Guido Reni was assessed at about 30 pounds.[25] This does not signify that stylistic parallels could be drawn between Bouguereau and Reni, on the one hand, and Van Eyck and Courbet on the other. At bottom, however, the reason for the differing judgments on the two Old Masters has as little to do with the styles of Reni and Van Eyck as admiration or rejection with the styles of Meissonier and Courbet.

For, strange as this may sound, what determined the conscious reaction of the public in both cases was very similar to what had evoked the reactions of the citizens of Siena, of Villon's mother, of Hans Fugger and of Louis XIV: the content, the subject matter of the representation, the (extra-artistic) "what" of the works, not the (artistic) "how."

In decisive contrast to the strata of the public of the past, however, the content of the representation of the works admired in the nineteenth century no longer bore any essential and genuine relation to those moral, religious, cultural, material, social and individual values which concretely determined the social and private life of the beholders. Moreover, a genuine essential relation between the paintings and the real life of the viewer not only no longer existed, but the viewer no longer even wanted such a relation. On the contrary, the more painters succeeded in evoking, through realistic details, the illusion of an undetermined, timeless, or long-passed "reality," remote from the "brute reality" in which the viewer lived, the better the work corresponded to his vague desire for something "higher," "interesting," "beautiful," "moving," or "edifying." In other words, art and works of art fulfilled functions for the new public which until then had not appertained to the primary functions of art because these functions in earlier times had been determined mostly by relatively small homogeneous groups within the public. The various strata of the public of earlier times were prepared, indeed they expected, to evaluate works of art as expressions of their own political, religious, and social aspirations of which they became more conscious precisely through this artistic representation. It was taken for granted that the works referred to their own social and private existence. The new public, however—Goethe's

25. Data from Kenneth Clark, "Art and Democracy," *Magazine of Art*, vol. 40, number 2 (Feb., 1947) pp. 74–79.

"motley crowd"—no longer wanted (consciously or unconsciously) this reference. In works of art they did not want to find the expression of the goals dominating the modern world and their own lives summarizable in the catchwords "free competition," "quantity," "production," "consumption," "profit," and "the acquisition of material goods." In short, works of art and artistic experience became separated from over-all experience, from the concrete existence of the viewer, and increasingly became an object of mere amusement, relaxation, recreation, a more or less dispensable ornament, a superfluity, and ceased to be an integral part of existence.

The spate of art scandals, however, that broke out in the middle of the nineteenth century (Courbet, Manet, Monet, *et al*) and continued till the turn of the century—which saw the acceptance of the Impressionists—attests that the conflict between the modern artists and the new public, evidenced in the cleavage between official and contested art, was still a genuine conflict, a conflict that is not to be dismissed out of hand with the customary remark about the uneducated philistines' bad taste or inability to understand art. Certainly, the reasons motivating the public were utterly non-artistic. But the conflict was a "genuine" art-conflict nevertheless in that the hostility and the scorn which greeted the modern masters unmistakably show that the ridiculed works were taken quite seriously and that the public, at bottom, sensed their dangerous power. To be sure, the wrath of the beholders, who had good reasons for not wanting to be reminded of modern reality, was aimed first of all at the subject matter of the pictures: Millet's "ugly" peasants, the banal "duck ponds" of the Barbizon painters, or Courbet's inelegant females ("farm horses" as the Empress Eugenie called them).

Yet this wrath and rejection indirectly and negatively conceded that the reality molded artistically in these pictures was not so easy to turn away from. For as long as this opposition between the content of the pictures and the demand that reality be embellished or forgotten existed and the impossibility of eluding the reality gave the beholders a sense of unease—however vague and on the surface—just as long did they protest against the pictures' claim to truth, grasped emotionally rather than intellectually, because it contained a critical element, and just as long did the conflict between the public and modern art remain a genuine art-conflict.[26]

The phase of such genuine conflict, however, now belongs to the past along with the great art scandals accompanying it and along with the age of liberalism in which they took place.

Whereas in today's situation, when art has become big business and an article of mass consumption, even the shrewdest publicity-minded managers of art have a hard time organizing a *succès de scandale.* For practically every "new" artist, without the benefit of "scandal," becomes through his sheer novelty a more or less short-lived success in the fashionable world (if only in terms of clever exhibition devices) and frequently the artist or his dealer enjoys a financial success.

At first glance, accordingly, the relation between the public and the contemporary artists seems to have undergone a fundamental change since the end of World War II. Indeed, the enormous growth of interest in art manifest in all highly industrialized countries—and most strikingly in the United States—during the last decades, can be easily shown by a brief listing of some well-known facts: the statistics on the number of visitors to museums and exhibitions run into millions, and everywhere in the Western hemisphere and in Europe during that period new museums have been (and continue to be) founded or existing ones enlarged. Various large international exhibitions dedicated to modern art such as the Biennale in Venice, the Triennale in Sao Paulo, the "Dokumenta" in Kassel, and the exhibitions assembled for the International Guggenheim Award in the New York museum of the same name invariably attract large crowds.

26. A deliberate distinction between "ideal" and "reality" and their evaluation as "untruth" or "truth" depending on the function of the picture is shown clearly in the following example, which is purposely taken not from the writings of an art critic but from an author who depicts in his novels the bourgeois middle class, which may be taken to be the "average" (English) public of his time. Anthony Trollope writes (in *The Last Chronicle of Barset*, Everyman's Library, vol. 2, p. 388): "We are, most of us, apt to love Raphael's madonnas better than Rembrandt's matrons. But, though we do so, we know that Rembrandt's matrons existed, but we have a strong belief that no such woman as Raphael painted ever did exist. In that he painted, as he may be surmised to have done, for pious purposes—at least for church purposes—Raphael was justified; but had he painted so for family portraiture he would have been false."

The record prices paid on the international art market for works of old and modern (still living!) artists, which are published not only in specialized journals but also in the daily press, shed light on another aspect of the generally expanded interest in art. Of course, to buy works of art as a "safe" capital investment, one of the main reasons for the current "art boom," cannot be compared with the motivations of the true collector. When a painting is purchased not as a work of art, however, but rather as a "commodity with a constant value"— and incidentally buyers and sellers today admit the commodity character of works of art far more candidly than was the case in the nineteenth century—this economic aspect considerably affects the nature of the general interest in art. (The influence exerted by the record price paid for a particular picture on the "art-judgment" of many contemporaries is probably similar to the influence exerted by the fame of a "miracle-working" image on its drawing power and evaluation in the past.)

Obviously, artistic interest in and enjoyment of works of art is not necessarily excluded by the fact that the works are bought or collected as capital investments, for purposes of speculation or, as so frequently in the United States for fiscal reasons.[27] At all events, the highly publicized prices certainly endow the possession of works of art with a social prestige which, although underlining the prestige of mere material wealth, nevertheless is of a quite different character. Whether ownership of works of art represents in the public consciousness (again especially in the United States) social "success" in the sense of a new synthesis of wealth, education, and culture, thereby spurring large segments of the middle class to follow suit, is a question that may be left open for the moment along with that of the role played in this context by the amazing growth and spread of amateur painting in the United States.[28] Here it suffices to note that at present there exists a very numerous public that in one way or another manifests its interest

27. The connection between the "boom" of the interest in art in the United States and the fiscal legislation adopted in 1939 and 1954, which made the purchase of works of art and their donation to cultural institutions a source of considerable tax reductions for the buyer, has not yet been studied with the thoroughness it merits.

28. According to *Preuves* (Dec. 1956) the number of amateur painters and sculptors in the United States in that year was estimated as ten million. (The same figure had already been cited in a speech by Dr. Gallan-

in painting and that buys pictures. Additional proof of the existence of such a public, excluded on economic grounds from the "big" international art market, is furnished by the many "art" galleries now mushrooming in almost all the big cities (and not only in tourist centers) which offer eager buyers pictures (not reproductions) on almost all price levels. Department stores have been selling pictures for several years now and as there are lending libraries, so are there institutions and stores that rent out paintings. It goes without saying that the great demand for paintings (or conversely the mass supply of "modern" paintings?) has thoroughly transformed the art dealer and collector of the old school. The largest and financially strongest firms with branches in all the important art centers or markets of Europe and America increasingly resemble industrial corporations in their structure and business methods and show similar monopolistic tendencies.[29]

This enumeration plus, in passing, the ever increasing number of art books published (with many reproductions and little text) clearly demonstrates the existence nowadays of a large public interested in painting and which, in contrast to the public of the nineteenth and early twentieth centuries, evinces no hostility at all toward contemporary painting.

Can this new situation be explained, and is it possible to eval-

---

tiere to the Congress of Museum Specialists and Art Historians on Jan. 6, 1954.)

In the same address, "Culture and Mass Culture in the United States," the speaker pointed out that sales of artists' supplies had risen from three million dollars in 1940 to forty million dollars in 1950. The National Art-Material Trade Association estimated in 1960 that the number of amateur painters had risen from thirty million in 1950 to forty million in 1960, of whom perhaps one million actually were taking instruction courses in painting. The newer figures are from A. Toffler, *The Culture Consumers: A Study of Art and Affluence in America* (New York: 1964) p. 20. The differences in the estimates can be explained by the fact that what is included as "artists' supplies" at any given time is not clear. For example, should number painting, which for a time was very popular, be included? This was an "artistic" leisure-time activity which consisted of painting one's own Van Gogh, Degas, or Gauguin by "oneself": a painting by one of the artists was printed in outline and the "original colors" to be filled in were indicated by numbers. The whole thing, however, was not intended for children but for adults!

29. Cf. H. Frank, *Die das 'Neue' nicht fuerchten!* (Duesseldorf-Vienna: 1964); see especially p. 266 ff.

uate its positive or negative significance with regard to the relation between artist and public or between contemporary society and art? To
the extent that the question concerns only the quantitative expansion
of the public this answer does not seem difficult: it is only today that
the mechanization and the "fragmentization" of labor[30] connected with
it has made possible, in all industrialized countries, that general extension of leisure time which constitutes the material precondition for
the rise of the modern "mass public" for whatever cultural sphere.

Set over against this result of technical civilization, however,
is the fact that the advanced mechanization of labor—*not technics as
such*—entails the destruction of the innermost emotional, psychic, and
intellectual preconditions without which a meaningful attitude in any
cultural sphere is impossible. For the at best impersonal relationship
of the worker to his mechanically regulated, repetitive, and always
fragmentary work-performance in the long run inevitably decreases
individual capacity for concentration, largely eliminates the possibility
of spontaneous (inner and outer) behaviour, and thwarts the development of independent judgment. In other words, the possibility for a
"mass public for art" follows all the less from the realized material
precondition of its existence inasmuch as the mental preconditions for
its coming into being are fundamentally menaced by the mechanization of labor. "Whatever its manifest content, mass culture must therefore not subvert the basic patterns of industrial life. Leisure time . . .
must provide relief from work monotony without making the return
to work too unbearable; it must provide amusement without insight
and pleasure without disturbance—as distinct from art which gives
pleasure through disturbance.

"To escape boredom and avoid effort is incompatible. . . . For
men molded in the image of contemporary society, art has many dangers: its effects are unpredictable and its demands tremendous. Art demands effort, a creative response from the audience."[31]

30. Georges Friedmann, *Le Travail en Miettes: Spécialisation et
Loisirs* (Paris: 1964); English translation, *The Anatomy of Work: Labor,
Leisure, and the Implications of Automation,* by Wyatt Rawson (New York:
Glencoe Free Press, 1962). This excellent book is the best *comprehensive* pre-
sentation and investigation of the effects of the mechanized labor process on
man in the so-called Western, that is, capitalist industrialized countries, which
are the only ones dealt with here.

31. Irving Howe, "Notes on Mass Culture," in *Mass Culture:
The Popular Arts in America,* ed. by B. Rosenberg and D. M. White (Glen-

Thus, it is not only the numerical growth of the public which explains its changed attitude toward contemporary art, as compared to the nineteenth century. Above all, this changed attitude is, at least in part, directly caused by the negative effects which the technologicalization of the labor process has on the human beings who individually and collectively constitute present-day mass society. Certainly art has "lost its sting" and has become a mere "by-product" of contemporary capitalist industrial society, into which neither works of art nor artists are "integrated."[32] But the generalized interest in art and the readiness with which today's public seems to accept modern painting also attests to the conscious or unconscious urge to flee from self-alienation and to still, with the help of art during leisure time, the need for more intimate participation, for making one's own choice, for "self-expression" and "self-assertion."

This does not signify, of course, that the individual motivations for the interest in art are the same in all those who make up the millions of museum visitors, amateur painters, etc. But whether the

coe, Ill.: 1960) pp. 497, 499. In the same volume, Melvin Tumin, "Popular Culture and the Open Society," p. 555: "Real creativity is viewed with suspicion and distrust because it means, above all, difference, intolerance, an insistence on achieving an individual identity. Real feeling is viewed with equal distrust and hostility because it almost always means bad manners, spontaneity, unpredictability, lack of realism, failure to observe routine. Above all, there is the question of form. One can't play it cool if he insists on the validity of his feelings. To play it hot is bad form." To give at least one example of the agreement prevailing among the most diverse authors, European and American, in their judgment of the negative effects of the modern division of labor, see Pierre Naville, "De l'Aliénation à la Jouissance," in *Le nouveau Leviathan*, vol. 1, *Recherches de Sociologie du Travail* (Paris: M. Riviere, 1957) p. 489: "Dans le monde actuel, il devient difficile d'affirmer que le loisir lui-même n'est pas, à certains égards, une forme de travail. Il l'est d'abord ... par son aspect directement productif; il l'est ensuite parce qu'il est tout orienté, surtout lorsqu'il est pratiqué en masse et par l'intermédiaire de ces *mass media* que sont les stades, les postes de radio et les écrans, vers la préparation du travail, vers la récupération des forces et du minimum d'équilibre indispensable à la bonne exécution du travail. Dans un système social que règle la nécessité de fer du travail, salarié ou autre, les périodes de détente ne peuvent être dans leur ensemble que des temps de préparation à l'effort productif. Le repos n'est que le maigre prix de l'épuisement, et la promesse d'une prochaine tension."

32. Wind, *Art and Anarchy*, p. 9; A. Gehlen, *Zeit-Bilder* (Frankfurt-Bonn: 1960) p. 222; J. Cassou, *Situation de l'Art Moderne* (Paris: 1950) pp. 101, 115.

contemporary attitude originates primarily in an inner reaction against the stultifying effects of mechanization or whether it serves the "tired businessman's" typical desire for relaxation, amusement, diversion, or, above all, pursuit of entirely different interests such as the furthering of social prestige or financial gain, at all events today's "hunger for art" seems, in its function, not to differ essentially from the interest in art exhibited by the "uncomprehending" "new" public at the end of the nineteenth and the beginning of the twentieth centuries.

Thus the question is all the more justified as to why today's public displays none of the resistance to contemporary art so clearly expressed in the former art scandals and in the cleavage between "official" and living art. The fact that the distinction between "official" and "avant-garde" painting has become meaningless—since all new (or pseudo-new) tendencies are immediately sanctioned by prominent buyers, museums, art critics, etc., whereby they become "official" for the general public—by itself underlines the change which has taken place in the relations between the public and art since the end of World War II. But is it a matter of fundamental or only of a gradual change in this relationship? Does the change rest primarily on a transformation of the public, of painting, or of both? Does today's public, for instance, differ from that of the second half of the nineteenth century in its structure (socially, educationally) or only in terms of its numbers? And is the painting of the last twenty-five years essentially the continuation of the artistic trends all of which found expression in the works of the "good old days" before World War II or even before World War I? Or is the public once more confronted by a painting that is as revolutionary and innovational in character as were the artistic revolutions exemplified by the opposition of Impressionism and Expressionism to Cubism and between Cubism and non-representational painting?

In evaluating today's changed relationship, the practical difficulties, within the framework of the present-day "art industry," besetting those who advocate views running counter to the convictions and interests of the artistically and financially most influential art dealers, museum directors, collectors, etc. must constantly be borne in mind. Equally significant is the proneness of people living in a mass society never to deviate from the opinion of the specialists who set the tone both with respect to general behaviour and questions of· art. ("Teacher, today again do we have to do what we want to do?"[33])

In short, the absence of art scandals or of a clearly articulated protest against the tendencies of contemporary art does not necessarily mean that today's public, which is either mute or cautiously keeping silent, actually views contemporary art with greater comprehension or more sincere acceptance than the pioneers of modern "anti-official" art were viewed by the loudly protesting opponents of their time.

This aspect of the current relation between public and painting is most clearly discernible in the United States, where the aforementioned growth of an art-interested public has been the most striking of all and has occurred at a truly galloping pace. Since the United States lacks a tradition of an artistically influential cultured middle class as well as a tradition in painting, such as existed, in however different forms, in European countries, this recent American "cultural explosion" cannot be considered a typical example of the artistic situation in the industrial countries of Europe. Its symptomatic significance, however, must be all the more emphasized because the United States and its much admired and much upbraided mass culture represent the most advanced stage of development of capitalist industrial societies.

It is hardly an accident that whereas the "culture consumers" of the typical mass media (film, radio, best sellers in records and books) have been analyzed with the utmost precision as to their occupation, age, income, etc., no thorough studies have been made regarding the social groups constituting the "mass public for painting" in the United States. The fact that the current art audience is indeed a new phenomenon in the United States does not sufficiently explain this lack of interest; nor does the fact that painting in its (superseded) traditional form of easel painting cannot be a mass medium in marked contrast to the graphic arts and to commercial art (posters, trademarks, packaging, etc.), without which contemporary man's daily life is unthinkable.

33. Quoted in David Riesman, *The Lonely Crowd* (Doubleday Anchor, 1956) p. 309.

Rather, the lack of scientifically reliable studies of the public for painting corresponds to the ratio of that public to the total population. In other words, the millions of museum visitors, buyers of paintings and reproductions, et al, are by no means a *mass audience* from the standpoint of the technological society and its "culture industries." In relation to the total population they are a numerical minority—the middle class that has achieved affluence.[34] "Despite the progress of [cultural] democratization, the fact remains that the mass of American workers and farmers are not participants in the culture boom.

"... there is little doubt that the worker and his family are badly under-represented in the total culture public. Similarly ... the number of Negroes in the culture audience is infinitesimal."[35]

Yet this purely statistical fact does not suffice to explain the minimal attention paid to the art audience (outside the circles directly involved, professionally and financially) because the social effect and importance of a (political, economic, etc.) minority is not determined by its numbers. A truer explanation lies rather in the fact that the independent cultural importance of this new art public is minimal since its artistic interests and needs spring to an even lesser degree from their own life-style than did those of the corresponding "new" groups in the public at the turn of the century in France or Germany, who followed the art judgments of the "official" authorities.

The far more unconditioned cultural dependency of the new American art public is attributable to the fact that the concept of social prestige is determined differently and more unequivocally in America

34. A. Toffler, *op. cit.*, emphasizes that the median income of this stratum of the public is fifty percent above the average income of the population as a whole.

35. *Ibid.*, pp. 35, 36. These statements are of a particular interest because nothing could be farther from the intentions of their author than a criticism of the present-day artistic situation in the United States. Rather, his whole effort is directed toward proving the success of the "democratization of the arts" since the end of World War II and toward prophesying the integration of art into society in the near future on the basis of progressive technologicalization: "We are busy freeing the arts in our society from their dependence upon a tiny, cult-like following. We are converting, as it were, from cult to culture" (p. 32). "For in that super-industrial civilization of tomorrow, with its vast, silent cybernetic intricacies and its liberating quantities of time for the individual, art will not be a fringe benefit for the few, but an indispensable part of life for the many. It will move from the edge to the nucleus of national life" (p. 68).

than in Europe. In the United States social prestige is a direct result of real economic success, manifested as property, possessions, etc., and fundamentally divorced from any concept of culture. Thus the attainment of such desired social prestige depends primarily, if not exclusively, on the extent to which an individual or a social group can afford to acquire those things the possession of which at any given time is considered as the undeniable mark (status symbol) of economic success. In contrast, in the eyes of the European middle-class public, owing to the vestiges of the system of "social estates" and feudal traditions, not only the "correct" things but also artists and intellectuals still possess a certain prestige which compensates for their economic powerlessness and accordingly endows the humanistic concept of culture with a precarious and relative value of its own foreign to the United States.

Simply for this reason perhaps the reaction of the general public to works of art in the various European countries is somewhat less uniform and less relentlessly subject to the whims of fashion than is that of the corresponding American public, which is prone to judge the value of a work of art by its price and its possession as a symbol of success. This is all the more understandable because American museums owe their existence almost exclusively to private financing and initiative and because the material wealth of the leaders in finance and industry is indeed inseparable from the artistic richness in which the public art collections abound.[36] But why is it that the number of visitors to museums in the United States has risen so enormously only in the last ten to fifteen years?

Although it does not offer a complete explanation for this phenomenon, the repercussions of the fiscal legislation of 1939 which were delayed by the war nevertheless provide a substantial part of the answer. For so long as only the wealthiest persons could afford to purchase valuable (European) paintings—and most of the works entered

36. Investments for cultural purposes (theater, music, museums, literature, etc.) by private institutions (foundations) came to more than thirty-three million dollars in 1965, that is, five percent of the total amount granted by foundations. Expenses by the American government for the arts in the same year were a little more than one cent per capita. Comparative figures for England, seventy United States cents per capita; Germany and France, twenty cents; Italy, sixteen cents. These figures are from a broadcast by Edward P. Morgan over the American Broadcasting Company radio network on April 11, 1966.

the public collections only after the deaths of their owners—the public for art remained preponderantly limited to the small intellectual segment of the middle class; the fabulous wealth of the purchasers of valuable paintings raised the works of art too into that rarefied and extraordinary sphere of life which seemed inaccessible to ordinary mortals. Today, however, the fiscal advantages make the purchase of paintings (and their donation to public institutions of culture) or the joint founding of new museums a rewarding investment for many affluent persons who are neither millionaires nor especially interested in art. Yet the more paintings bought—for whatever reasons—during the last decades found their way into museums, the more did this very fact enhance the prestige of their donors, and all the more did the interest in art become a matter affecting ever wider circles among the same affluent middle-class strata.

By the force of circumstances those buyers had no choice but to turn their interest toward contemporary painting since old masters as well as the modern classics (Manet, Cézanne, etc.) became increasingly rarer on the market and therefore were available only at higher and higher prices. Furthermore, contemporary and above all "new" painters offered greater possibilities for speculation since prices rise almost automatically if the work of a still unpromoted artist is acquired for the permanent collection of a museum as influential as the Museum of Modern Art in New York or is shown in an exhibition arranged by this institution. It does not matter that the financial value thus achieved may be short-lived since the museum deliberately attributes less importance to the inherent artistic quality of the picture than to its topical value—the picture as a document of the artistic action of the immediate present.[37]

37. This attitude on the part of museum administrators is expressed most clearly in Alfred H. Barr's original formulations of the museum's goals in 1942, the continuing validity of which, however, was again emphasized by the museum directors in 1966: "The Museum is aware that it may often guess wrong in its acquisitions. When it acquires a dozen recent paintings it will be lucky if in 10 years, three will still seem worth looking at, if in 20 years only one should survive. For the future, the important problem is to acquire this one: the other nine will be forgiven—and forgotten. But meanwhile we live in the present, and for the present these other nine will seem just as necessary and useful, serving their purpose by inclusion in exhibitions here and on tour, so long as their artistic lives shall last.

Of course it would be absurd to contend that the new American public of the affluent middle class consists exclusively of people who consider paintings above all, or even exclusively, as objects of profitable financial investment or speculations. Undoubtedly, however, this economic aspect contributed decisively to establishing a close bond between interest in art and social prestige, so that interest in art has now become a social "must" for these middle-class strata—something that "one" must do if "one" wants to be counted as part of the "in-group." In addition, this economic aspect helped further to promote the general interest in contemporary painting, which is the "official" art of today. The conclusion that the present-day public possesses a deeper understanding of art because the now "official" contemporary art is (at least partially) "better" and artistically "more honest" than the art produced by the painters in vogue at the end of the nineteenth century is therefore inadmissible.

When Max Liebermann painted the little daughter of a Berlin museum director, Wilhelm von Bode, the child looked at the picture and asked the artist, "Is the picture finished now?" Upon being told that it was, she went on to ask, "Will it go into papa's museum now?" "Yes," said Liebermann. "And will it have a gold frame around it?" Liebermann answered that the picture would indeed be framed, whereupon she asked, "And will it become beautiful then?"

This is a question that would not be asked by the very numerous members of today's public for whom visits to museums and art galleries, lecture series and courses on art have become a new injunction which they observe for the sake of prestige as conscientiously as the corresponding material obligations with regard to the choice of the "right" car, the "right" residential area, although they proceed from the same (utterly groundless) assumption that a picture is good because it hangs in a museum. But if they don't "like" the newest paintings (or like them much less than the public liked the Bouguereaus and Cabanels, who were preferred to Courbet, Manet, and Van Gogh), they will be careful not to say so aloud, either because they do not trust their own judgment or in order to avoid committing an embarrassing

---

Sooner or later time will eliminate them." From a press release by the Museum of Modern Art, April 6, 1966.

social blunder. In contrast, the public of the nineteenth century could express its dislike of the avant-garde of its time all the more unguardedly inasmuch as by these protests it was but following the judgments of the "fashionable" world as handed down through press reviews, the purchases by public institutions, the "Prix de Rome," or the high prices paid. The choice of being for or against the official art no longer exists, even theoretically, for the corresponding group of today's public, because no avant-garde in contradistinction to the official art exists any more.[38]

But has not the relation to painting of those members of the new public whose interest in art is not primarily oriented toward superficialities but springs, instead, from an inner need undergone a decisive transformation? And does not the clearest proof of such a transformation lie in the fact that this inner need is gratified by contemporary painting?

Though only the works of the younger and youngest generation of artists—the successors of Kandinsky, Delaunay, Malevich, Mondrian—posit the cleavage existing today between the social and private being of men as a matter of course, the devaluation of man in capitalist industrial society is nevertheless already expressed in the radiantly shimmering works of the Impressionists, in which human figures, telegraph poles, and grass are no longer distinguished from each other. Painting, in its development from the Impressionists to today, shows no fundamental change in this respect. Rather, it reflects with increasing clarity the ever deeper self-alienation ensuing from the specialization of labor, carried to the highest degree. The devaluation of the social significance of a work of art as a possible expression of a destroyed or longed-for human community necessarily ran parallel to this development. On the other hand, it helped to strengthen the hedonistic function of the individual enjoyment of art—as effortless relaxation, diversion, satisfaction of sentimental or emotional needs. Whereas this function remained the same for the nineteenth-century and the present-day public, the manner of its fulfillment has undergone a crucial change. As regards the admirers of the works of the formerly fashionable painters, their enjoyment of art had been essentially

38. See the editorial in the *Burlington Magazine*, vol. XCVIII, no. 627 (June, 1955) "The Contemporary Situation."

determined by the fact and the degree to which pictures afforded them the opportunity to escape from themselves and from existing social reality. Conversely, the enjoyment of art experienced by the self-alien-ated persons of today depends above all on the degree and the im-mediacy with which they can identify with a work, that is, the degree to which the work of art furthers self-assertion.

The nineteenth-century admiration for the dishonest pictures still contained, however dimly and distortedly, the admission that the world and the people in it are not as they ought to be, even if the suc-cess of the pictures rested precisely on their ability to conceal this fact.

Since the members of today's public are supposedly not fleeing from themselves but hope, rather, to find in the picture their own identity and the possibility of a "self-expression" otherwise denied them, it is an indispensable and basic precondition that the work of art must impose no restraining force of any kind to which the beholder must submit—be it no more than the hint of the difference between that which is and that which could be (no longer: what "ought to be"). "The worst picture can speak to the sensibility and the imagination by setting them into motion and making them free and autonomous; the best work of art also speaks to the sensibility, but in a loftier language which, to be sure, one must understand; it fetters the feelings and the imagination; it robs us of our arbitrary will; we cannot do as we like with perfection; we are forced to surrender to it, so that it may lead us back to ourselves, enhanced and improved." (Goethe)[39]

Thus, the contemporary works of the most recent past (about the last twenty years) are all the more bound to correspond to the self-alienated beholder because even the (formally) best of them, in accordance with their subjective and fragmentary nature, can indeed arouse the beholder's imagination, his sensibility, and his arbitrariness but cannot lead him in any definite direction. For this very reason the beholder can by no means "surrender" himself to the painting. Rather, he can only project himself into the work. It is obviously impossible for him to achieve a deeper self-knowledge in this way, to say nothing of a return to himself "enhanced and improved." On the other hand, in fact, the painting affords him a liberating illusion of genuine spon-taneity: the work stimulates him to give free rein to his imagination

39. Introduction to the first volume of the *Propylaeen*, 1798.

and emotions to the extent that he is able to do so, a luxury which everyday life denies him.

The "self-expression" afforded him by contemporary painting is, no doubt, beneficial to the self-alienated beholder; it provides that self-assertion without self-knowledge of which he is needful. The same desire for self-expression and self-assertion (and not an authentic "craving for culture") also explains the millions of amateur painters in America.

Despite all the talk about the search for identity the hedonistic function of art in present-day industrial society seems to consist precisely in avoiding the beholder's consciousness of his self-alienation and, instead, in asserting this alienation in the semblance of self-expression.